Wealth Is Simple to Elevate

7 Steps to Master Cash Flow and Build Lasting Wealth

Maria James

Empower Wealth Publishing

For permissions contact:
Pocket of Money, LLC info@pocketofmoney.com

For information about special discounts available for bulk purchases, sales promotions, fund-raising, and educational needs, contact the author, Maria James, at 443-304-8896 or info@pocketofmoney.com. Website: www.pocketofmoney.com

Published by Empower Wealth Publishing.

Table of Contents

Introduction

I remember standing in my bathroom one morning, toothbrush in hand, staring up at the ceiling as another chunk of plaster gave way and crashed into the tub. It wasn't the first time it had happened. The bathroom ceiling was slowly caving in (for the third time), and so was my patience.

Every time this happened, I'd call maintenance again. They'd promise to fix it "soon." I could barely use my bathroom, but I had to wait for maintenance to patch the two-foot hole in the ceiling right above the tub ... again. Finally, it would get fixed, and then a couple of weeks later, it would cave in again, water pouring into my apartment. The hole stared at me and reminded me daily that I was paying too much rent to feel so uncomfortable in my own home.

After I was told to "just use the sink", that's when I decided *enough was enough.*

I wasn't going to renew my lease, but I had a few months to find a new apartment, maybe even buy my first home. I wanted to do research first before pulling the plug, but life was hectic when the deadline came ... and I missed it by one day. Just one.

The penalty? $1,600.

I stared at that number in disbelief. That money could've gone toward a down payment or the moving expenses I knew were coming. Instead, it vanished in a single moment of delay. For someone living off less than $3,000 a month after taxes, that felt like a small earthquake in my financial world.

I remember sitting there after the company gave me the fee, just staring at the number in the email. My mind raced through the usual questions: Do I put it on a credit card? Delay it and risk more fees? Pull from my savings and have to work to replace it?

It was a defining moment, not just because I had to make a quick decision, but because I realized something deeper: life doesn't wait for you to "get ready." Emergencies don't schedule themselves around payday. And if you don't have systems in place to manage your money, one unexpected expense can spiral into months (or years) of financial stress.

That day, I chose to use my emergency fund. It wasn't easy watching my savings dip, but I felt something I didn't think I would feel: peace. I didn't have to panic, borrow, or beg. I handled the problem and kept moving forward. That experience embodies everything I teach today.

I saw the same pattern play out in people around me, friends, colleagues, and clients, making good money but still one crisis away from financial chaos. Some were furloughed during economic downturns. Others faced flooded homes, medical bills, or months where income suddenly dried up. Each time, I was reminded: wealth

8

isn't just about having money; it's about having control and the financial success to be flexible.

In my story, it wasn't just about the lease. It was about control and flexibility. That $1,600 mistake drove home a truth I'd known for years but now felt deep in my bones: **your money choices determine how much freedom you have.** If I hadn't built up savings and managed my cash flow, that fee could've derailed my entire plan to move. I would have been stuck in a pretty unhealthy and potentially risky environment. Emergencies don't always look like job loss or medical bills. Sometimes, they're small moments that carry big financial consequences.

It was an important reminder and became a turning point. I realized that money management isn't just about budgeting. It's about *options*. It's about having the freedom to say, "I don't have to stay here." The freedom to choose safety, comfort, and opportunity instead of settling for stress and uncertainty.

Wealth, to me, isn't about luxury cars or designer handbags. It's about peace. It's about having a cushion when life happens and the ability to build something lasting for your family and your community. It's about knowing that when ceilings cave in, literally or figuratively, your finances don't have to collapse too.

That's why I wrote this book.

I want you to experience that kind of freedom. I want you to build wealth that goes beyond survival, the kind that helps you live comfortably, invest in others, and create a legacy that lasts for generations.

Money management and wealth building aren't luxuries for "later." They are survival skills for today and legacy tools for tomorrow. When you understand your cash flow, when you build your emergency fund, when you invest wisely and with intention, you're not just buying yourself comfort, you're buying your freedom. You're buying the ability to protect your family, to invest in your community, and to pass something forward besides stress.

Financial stability isn't about being lucky or brilliant. It's about being intentional. I want you to see what's possible, not just when you make more money, but when you master it.

So, let's begin because your financial future doesn't start when the world is calm. It starts the moment you decide to take control, right in the middle of life's chaos.

How Money Habits Shape Stress and How Stress Shapes Your Life
I would be remiss if I didn't touch on financial stress and its significant impact.

Financial stress is not just a money issue. It is a full-body, full-mind experience that quietly erodes a person's health and quality of life. When someone worries about bills, debt, or not having enough, their nervous system interprets that uncertainty as danger. The body reacts as if facing a threat, releasing stress hormones like cortisol and adrenaline.

Over time, this constant state of alert takes a physical toll. Sleep becomes disrupted as the mind races at night, leaving the body exhausted and less able to recover. Muscles tighten in the shoulders, neck, and jaw, causing chronic tension and headaches. Prolonged stress also raises blood pressure and strains the cardiovascular system, increasing the risk of hypertension and heart disease. Even digestion suffers as stress affects appetite and the gut, leading to overeating, loss of appetite, or persistent digestive discomfort. Eventually, the immune system weakens, making a person more susceptible to illness and slower to heal.

The mental and emotional toll can be just as significant. Financial stress often triggers persistent anxiety, creating a cycle of worry over "what if" scenarios that make it difficult to focus or make decisions. Over time, this can lead to feelings of hopelessness or depression, where motivation fades, and responsibilities feel overwhelming. The constant pressure drains mental energy, resulting in decision fatigue. The brain simply becomes too overwhelmed to plan, prioritize, or manage money effectively. This can lead to avoidance, missed payments, or impulsive financial choices that worsen the situation. Shame often follows, as people privately blame themselves for their struggles and feel embarrassed or "behind" compared to others. Relationships also suffer; financial stress increases conflict, reduces emotional connection, and turns ordinary conversations into arguments.

When you understand how deeply financial stress affects both the body and the mind, it becomes clear that managing money isn't just about building wealth; it's about protecting your health, your relationships, and your overall well-being. Good financial habits bring more than financial stability. They restore peace of mind. They help you sleep better, think more clearly, and show up more fully in your life. Mastering your money is not simply a financial goal. It is an essential part of caring for yourself.

Financial stress is not simply about a lack of money. It's about lack of margin, lack of clarity, and lack of control. And nothing influences those three things more than your money management habits.

Why Habits Matter More Than Income

I've coached people who made six figures but were drowning in stress and others who earned average incomes but felt steady, confident, and capable of handling whatever came.

The difference? Habits.

Good money habits, such as saving consistently, automating bills, and tracking spending, create a financial ecosystem where stress has fewer places to hide. These small, steady actions build predictability, and predictability builds peace.

Poor habits, on the other hand, invite chaos. When you don't know how much money is coming in or going out, every unexpected expense feels like a crisis. Every decision feels urgent. Every bill feels personal. Financial stress doesn't gradually creep into your life; it barges in.

The Weight Money Stress Puts on Your Life
When people describe financial stress, they usually talk about the numbers: the bills, the income, the debt. However, the real impact shows up in quieter, more painful ways:

- You lose sleep. You lie awake wondering how you'll stretch the next paycheck.
- You lose focus. Financial worry eats up mental bandwidth. You're at work, but your mind is doing math.
- You lose your patience. Money anxiety spills into your relationships in the form of short tempers and long silences.
- You lose confidence. Opportunities start to feel threatening instead of exciting.
- You lose your spark. The joy you once had for hobbies, vacations, and dreaming gets replaced by survival mode.

And survival mode is exhausting.

For many people, financial stress becomes a background noise so constant that they don't notice how deeply it's affecting them. They think they're just "tired" or "unmotivated," when in reality they're carrying the emotional equivalent of a 50-pound weight in their chest every single day.

Here's the Truth and Hope

Money stress is not a life sentence. You can interrupt the financial stress cycle. You can build money management habits that support you, financial systems that protect you, and routines that restore your sense of control.

I've seen it happen over and over again. Take *"Jasmine,"* a blend of real clients, a woman who avoided her credit card statements because even the envelope made her stomach twist. She started small: $10 a week into savings, automated. Next, she wrote down her debts and implemented a debt elimination strategy. Slowly, the numbers shifted. But something else shifted, too.
She slept better.
She laughed more.
Her relationships improved.
She began to feel hopeful again, something she hadn't felt in years.

That is what good money habits do. Good money management habits don't just change your bank account. They change your life.

The Power of Money Management: Why It's Essential for Financial Success

Money touches every aspect of our lives. It dictates the opportunities we can pursue, the security we feel, and the legacy we leave behind. Yet, personal finance is often viewed as confusing, overwhelming, or something to be tackled "later." However, the truth is, financial success isn't about luck or solely based on how much money you make. Many people struggle with money management, financial stress, living paycheck to paycheck, or failing to reach their financial goals. This is not because they don't earn enough, but because they don't have a **clear and effective money management system**.

This book is designed to simplify personal finance and provide a clear roadmap to financial stability and wealth creation. Whether you're just starting your financial journey or looking to optimize your current situation, this book will walk you through practical, actionable steps to take control of your money.

Succeeding at money management isn't about being wealthy. It's about being intentional with your financial choices so you can build security, reduce stress, and create opportunities for yourself, your family, and your community. It's about financial control, security, and freedom, the ability to make choices that align with your values and aspirations. Here's why mastering money management and establishing a strong financial system is crucial for long-term success.

Financial Security and Stability

One of the most significant benefits of effective money management is achieving **financial stability**. Without a plan, unexpected expenses can send your finances into chaos. When you know how to budget, save, and plan for the future, you're less likely to live paycheck to paycheck. You're more likely to be able to build wealth.

A **solid money management system** ensures you cover all your essential expenses, such as housing, food, and transportation, without struggling.

The purpose of an **emergency fund** is to cover unexpected expenses and prevent financial crises. Life is unpredictable, and emergencies can happen at any time. Having savings set aside ensures that a car repair, appliance replacement, home repair, medical bill, or job loss doesn't cause a financial disaster.

You reduce debt stress by managing and eliminating high-interest liabilities and avoiding debt traps. Money problems are one of the leading causes of stress. Financial uncertainty can strain relationships, impact mental health, and even affect work performance. Poor financial planning often leads to reliance on credit cards and loans, trapping you in a cycle of debt. A strong money management system ensures that you're living within your means and paying off debts strategically.

Sleep peacefully. Financial stress is one of the leading causes of anxiety. When you have a system in place, you can stop worrying about whether you'll have enough money to pay all your bills and still enjoy life.

Feel **empowered** knowing you're in control of your money. Gain **confidence** in making financial decisions. With financial stability, you don't have to worry about sudden emergencies derailing your life because you have a safety net in place.

Achieving Your Financial Goals

Financial success does not happen by accident. It's intentional. Whether you want to buy a home, start a business, retire early or comfortably, or travel the world, the achievement of your financial goals depends on how well you manage your money. Without a system in place, your dreams may remain just that, dreams. A comprehensive money management system allows you to:

Create a structured financial plan that helps you set clear financial goals and break them down into achievable steps. Instead of vague wishes like "I want to save more," you'll have specific goals such as "I will save $10,000 for a home down payment in two years."

Budgeting and saving are important tools for achieving milestones like homeownership, investing, and financial independence. You can track progress and adjust your strategy when needed, ensuring you stay on course.

You will make Smarter Investments.
With your finances in order, you can confidently invest in opportunities that grow your wealth instead of making impulsive financial decisions.

An effective money management system turns financial dreams into actionable plans. When you have a clear plan, you stop worrying about money and start using it as a tool for empowerment. Without an effective system, money tends to control you instead of the other way around. You may find yourself wondering, "Where did my paycheck go?" every month. However, when you take charge of your finances, you dictate how your money is spent, saved, and invested.

Creating Wealth and Financial Freedom
Good money management is not just about covering expenses or paying bills. It's about building wealth and financial freedom. Without a plan, money flows in and out without growing. However, when managed correctly, money works for you to build wealth.

- **Investing wisely** allows your money to grow over time, creating long-term wealth.
- **Debt reduction strategies** free up more income for savings and investments.
- **Smart financial decisions** compound over time, leading to cash flow optimization and financial independence.

Financial freedom means you no longer rely solely on a paycheck. You have assets and investments working for you to increase funds.

Preparing for the Future and Leaving a Legacy of Wealth

Financial success isn't just about handling today's finances. It's about building a secure future for yourself and your family. This is why you need those assets and investments. Poor money management keeps you stuck, only able to handle bills, and can lead to financial hardship later in life, forcing you to work longer, be trapped in a never-ending debt cycle, or rely on others for support.

- **Retirement Planning** – The earlier you start saving and investing for retirement, the more time your money has to grow. A good financial system ensures you're consistently contributing to retirement accounts.
- **Wealth Protection** – Having the right insurance, estate planning, and emergency funds protects your wealth from unforeseen circumstances.
- **Generational Wealth** – By managing your money well, you can create financial security not just for yourself, but for future generations.
- **Estate planning** – This ensures your wealth benefits your loved ones.
- **Financial literacy** – Knowledge is one of the greatest assets and, when passed on to children, creates a culture of financial success.

- **Smart investing** – This allows your wealth to grow across generations and creates opportunities for future generations to thrive rather than struggle

Preparing for the Unexpected

Once you have a system and are working on growing assets, you don't want one event to be able to disrupt everything. Life is unpredictable. Job losses, medical emergencies, and economic downturns happen. A strong money management system ensures you're prepared for whatever life throws your way.

- **Insurance and wills** protect your family and assets.
- **An emergency fund** covers unexpected expenses without derailing your financial goals.
- **Multiple income streams** provide security in uncertain times.

By managing your money wisely, you **reduce financial vulnerability** and protect your future from financial disaster. We'll go deeper later.

What You'll Learn

Now that you understand why money management is essential, you're ready to learn how you can build a system that works. By the end of this book, you will have a WISE action plan and reset protocol to create a great money management system that will empower you to

- design financial goals that will create your desired lifestyle,

- achieve those goals,
- progress with wealth building, and
- protecting that wealth to leave a legacy of wealth.

We begin by understanding your financial status, taking a financial snapshot, and reviewing key financial status indicators, such as your credit report. Once you know where you stand, we'll guide you through building a strong financial system with organized documents and an effective financial plan. However, numbers alone don't create wealth. Your beliefs and mindset also matter. We'll explore the beliefs and habits that shape financial success and how to develop a wealth-building mentality.

With the right foundation in place, we move into strategic financial planning: setting clear financial goals, creating a budget that works, and learning how to stick to it. You'll also discover how to spend wisely and embrace frugality without feeling deprived. No financial plan is complete without a strong savings strategy. Whether you're saving for emergencies, major purchases, or future investments, this chapter will help you create a system that works for you.

Debt can be a major obstacle, but it doesn't have to be permanent. We'll break down the credit-debt cycle, understanding credit reports, and multiple debt elimination strategies so you can free yourself from financial stress.

Protecting your wealth is just as important as building it. We'll discuss the necessary elements to ensure that you're protecting your wealth and securing your and your family's financial future.

Finally, we'll dive into investing: why it's essential, how to prepare, different investment vehicles, and how to start building wealth. Even if you've never invested before, this section will help you take the first steps with confidence.

How to Use This Book
Each chapter is designed to be practical and easy to follow, with step-by-step guidance and actionable strategies. You don't have to read it all at once, start where you need the most help, implement what you learn, and revisit sections as your financial situation evolves.

Taking control of your finances isn't about perfection. It's about progress. With consistency, the right knowledge, and a plan tailored to your life, you can build financial security and create a lasting legacy of wealth.

Money isn't just a tool. It's a foundation for your future. Succeeding at money management isn't about restricting yourself or obsessing over every dollar. It's about creating a system that allows you to live with financial confidence and freedom. By taking control of your money today, you set yourself up for less or no financial stress and a prosperous future ... one where you can enjoy life, seize opportunities, and leave a lasting financial legacy. Start managing your money wisely and watch how it transforms your life.

Step 1: The Organization Blueprint

Chapter 1: Assess Financial Status

Financial status refers to your current state of financial well-being. Think of it as your "money situation." Often, people use words such as broke, well-off, rich, or wealthy to describe a person's financial status or well-being. Financial well-being has three core stages or phases: stability, security, and freedom. We don't normally think about it in these terms. We normally think about the ways that it shows up in or affects our lives.

Financial status affects where you can live, what type of food and how much food you can buy, what type of transportation you can have, e.g., public transportation or a car, where you can send your children for daycare and school, and more.

Your financial status affects your financial stress levels and your physical and mental health. For many of us, it also significantly affects our sense of self-worth, confidence, and identity.

You're working on elevating your financial status. Well, the first step to do that is to understand what each of the three phases looks like, so you can clearly see in which phase you fall.

The first phase is **financial stability**. This is when your current financial status is stable. This means that
- Your monthly income can cover your monthly expenses.
- There are no bills past due.

- You can save a portion of your income.
- You can afford to purchase wants, items beyond necessities.

The second phase or stage is **financial security**. This is when you can handle current bills and long-term expenses and contribute money towards financial goals. You are likely aggressively working on all or a combination of the items below.

- Saving to establish or complete an emergency fund.
- Saving to purchase a high-cost item.
- Eliminating debt.
- Investing for retirement.
- Investing in non-retirement accounts.

The third and final phase or stage is **financial freedom**. Financial freedom can look and feel different depending on your risk tolerance. However, the following items are usually accomplished.

- You've fully funded an emergency fund.
- You have little to no high-interest debt.
- You're able to live your desired lifestyle.

To accurately determine your financial stage, you need to learn and assess key financial status indicators. These numbers help inform your level of financial fitness and provide more clarity than the yes-or-no situational questions above. They also standardize your financial data so that anyone, e.g., a lender or advisor, can look at your data and explain how you compare and if you're on track with your financial goals.

What's the destination?

Think about when you have to take a trip to a new place. Somewhere you've never been. Consider the actions you take to make the trip successful. You consider the weather and what clothes and supplies you need to pack. You determine various routes and methods of transportation and pick the best one. You research activities and consider meals to design a budget for the trip. These are just a few of the actions you may take to plan a successful trip to a new place.

Planning financial goals is similar to planning a trip. The starting point, the destination, the research, and the preparation are crucial for success.

To write financial goals that are relevant and allow you to progress through the financial stages, you have to be clear on your starting point, i.e., your current financial status. Do the research and get the necessary knowledge to design an effective strategic plan.

WISE Score
Understanding Your WISE™ Financial Fitness Score

To help you clearly see where you stand and what steps will move you forward, I created the **WISE™ Financial Fitness Score**, a simple, proprietary, comprehensive assessment designed to measure your financial health with the same clarity and confidence that a credit score provides for your borrowing history.

Think of your WISE score as your personal financial pulse check. It looks beyond income and assets and gives you a full picture of how well your behaviors, mindset, and accomplishments work together to build long-term financial success.

What the WISE™ Financial Fitness Assessment Measures

Your WISE score is built from three powerful components that influence your financial outcomes more than anything else:

1) Behavior (55%) — What You Do With Your Money

This is the strongest predictor of your financial success. Behavior includes your daily money habits, such as budgeting, tracking spending, saving consistently, making on-time payments, managing debt, and preparing for emergencies. These are the actions that shape your financial reality.

2) Mindset (30%) — How You Think About Money

Your beliefs drive your decisions. This section measures things like:

- whether you believe you can build wealth
- your confidence in managing money
- your relationship with spending and saving

- how you handle financial stress
- your willingness to plan ahead

A strong mindset makes powerful habits possible.

3) Accomplishments (15%) — What You've Already Built

These are milestones that show the progress you've made so far, such as having an emergency fund, saving for retirement, paying down debt, increasing your net worth, or managing credit responsibly.

Even small accomplishments count. They are the proof that you're moving in the right direction.

What Your WISE™ Score Means

Your final WISE score is calculated on a scale of **0 to 100**. It reflects your overall financial fitness. The same way your physical health might be measured through strength, flexibility, and endurance.

Here's how to interpret your score:

90–100: Excellent Financial Fitness

You're in a strong financial position with healthy habits and a solid foundation. Keep going—your behaviors and mindset are aligned with long-term wealth building.

75–89: Good

You're doing many things well. A few key adjustments can elevate you into excellent territory and help you build wealth faster and more consistently.

60–74: Fair

You have strengths, but also several gaps holding you back. With targeted improvements to your habits or mindset, you can transform your financial stability within months.

40–59: Vulnerable

Financial stress is likely showing up in your decisions, household, or mental bandwidth. This is the time to rebuild your foundation, starting with better money management behaviors and small wins.

Below 40: Critical

You're likely facing financial instability, uncertainty, or chronic stress. But here's the good news: this score gives you clarity. It pinpoints exactly where to start, and every upward step will bring meaningful relief and improvement.

How to Use Your WISE™ Score in the App

Inside the WISE Pocket of Money App, your score becomes a financial roadmap personalized for you.

You'll be able to:
- See your strengths and weaknesses instantly.
- Identify the specific behaviors or beliefs holding you back.
- Get tailored action steps based on your score.
- Track your progress over time.
- Celebrate your accomplishments as your score increases.

31

The more honest you are in the assessment, the more precise and powerful your recommendations will be.

Think of your WISE score as your GPS for wealth-building. It doesn't judge you. It simply tells you where you are and then shows you the easiest path forward.

Why This Matters

Most people know they want to "get better with money," but they don't know *where to begin*. The WISE Financial Fitness Assessment removes the guesswork. It gives you:

- Clarity
- Direction
- Personalized insight
- And measurable progress.

You can't fix what you can't see. Your WISE score makes the invisible visible so you can build wealth with intention, strategy, and confidence.

The initial WISE Financial Fitness Score shows your current baseline financial fitness. However, other specific financial status indicators should still be reviewed, such as net worth, credit score, debt-to-income ratio, and more. You've already gotten your WISE Score, so now we're going to take a look at your other financial status indicators. [*If you haven't already, take time out to calculate your WISE Score. Go to the resources page: pocketofmoney.com/wise-resources*]

Net Worth

Net worth is a measure of wealth. It's what an individual owns, minus what is owed to others. Put another way, it's assets (what is owned) minus liabilities (what is owed or debts).

Have you seen articles that list the world's millionaires and billionaires? Those articles refer to an individual's net worth. The number listed is not the amount of money they have in the bank. It is the value of their assets minus their liabilities. Their assets are in the millions or billions, and even after subtracting their debts, their net worths are in the millions or billions.

Seems amazing, right? The good thing is the formula for building wealth isn't a secret. The formula for net worth is net worth equals assets minus liabilities.

$$Net\ worth = Assets - Liabilities$$

Let's break down this formula.

Assets vs. True Assets

An asset is something you own that can be sold for money. A true asset you own outright (you don't owe money on it at all), and it appreciates (increases in value). The asset will be worth more money as time goes by not less.

Let's go over some examples. We'll start with some of the most expensive things the average person owns. Many people will preach to you that your house is an asset. In the strict sense of the word, yes, it is. However, when you're still paying a mortgage on it and you have less equity in it than what you owe on it, it's not a true asset.

Your car is not a true asset. Again, in the strictest sense of the word, yes, you could sell your car for cash, but you will not get anywhere near what you paid for it. A car depreciates over time, meaning it's worth less and less money as time goes on. Consider your car a liability.

Other assets that you've likely heard of when discussing investing are stocks and bonds. Any investments you have in the stock market or bonds are considered assets. These are true assets as they are likely to increase in value over time … provided you don't sell when the market dips or it was a generally bad investment from the start.

Liabilities
Liabilities are what you owe; in other words, your debts. You can see a list of your liabilities (excluding household bills and money not borrowed from a lending institution) on your credit report. You can use credit monitoring sites to see everything that has been reported to credit bureaus on your credit report. A credit bureau is a company/agency that collects your loan data from

34

creditors or lenders. This is the data used to calculate your credit score.

Determine your total liabilities (debts you owe) and your total assets (items you own). Use those numbers to calculate your net worth. This will provide a good, quick snapshot of your financial situation. However, we're not done yet. Let's go over a few additional factors.

Interpret Your Net Worth
Net Worth:
You've added up your assets. You've totaled your debts. You've run the numbers and determined your net worth. Now comes the most important part: understanding what that figure actually tells you about your financial health.

Let's break it down.

1) Negative, Zero, or Positive
The first question to answer is simple: *Is your net worth negative, zero, or positive?*

Negative Net Worth
If your total debts exceed your total assets, your net worth will be negative, meaning you owe more than you own. This is extremely common, especially if you've pursued higher education and carry student loans, or if you have a mortgage, car loans, or medical debt.

A negative net worth doesn't mean you're failing financially. It simply means your next steps are clear:

- **Decrease your liabilities** by paying down debt.
- **Increase your assets** by saving and investing in things that grow in value.

Zero or Low Positive Net Worth

If you're hovering around zero or just slightly in the positive range, you're in a stronger position but still building your foundation. Your focus now is to:

- **Pay off** remaining debts.
- **Protect and maintain** the assets you have.
- **Continue accumulating** new assets that support long-term wealth.

Positive Net Worth

If your assets exceed your liabilities, you're moving in the right direction. The higher your net worth, the greater your financial flexibility and security. Stay intentional by:

- Keeping debt low or eliminating it entirely.
- Consistently acquiring and growing productive assets.
- Making sure your money is working just as hard as you are

2) Good for Your Age

A standalone net worth number doesn't mean much without context. Compare it to where you *need* to be based on your long-term goals, especially your retirement goals.

Ask yourself:

- Am I on track to reach the amount I'll need by my target retirement age?
- Does my current net worth align with the future lifestyle I'm planning?

If your net worth puts you on pace for those goals, you're in a strong position. If not, even if your net worth is technically positive, you'll need to increase your savings rate, invest more consistently, or adjust your financial strategy so you can get back on track.

3) Why Net Worth Isn't the Whole Story

Your net worth gives you a powerful snapshot of your overall financial position, but it's still just one metric. It's important to analyze the components separately as well as your savings habits, debt levels, cash flow, retirement contributions, and investment growth. They all influence long-term wealth.

Think of your net worth as your financial dashboard: one quick glance tells you where you stand, but deeper analysis helps you understand *why* you're there and *what to do next.*

Debt-to-Income Ratio

Your **debt-to-income ratio (DTI)** is a snapshot of how much of your monthly income is already committed to debt payments. It compares the total of your required monthly debt payments, such as credit cards, student loans, auto loans, personal loans, and mortgages, to your gross monthly income. The formula is: Debt-to-income Ratio equals total monthly debt payments divided by total gross monthly income.

$$DTI = \frac{Total\ montly\ debt\ payments}{Total\ gross\ monthly\ income}$$

Your total monthly debt payments are the total of all the minimum payments for all your debt accounts. Your total gross monthly income is the amount of money you earn before taxes. It's reflected on your pay stub.

I suggest you modify the traditional equation to this:

Debt-to-income ratio = total monthly debt payments / total net monthly income.

$$DTI = \frac{Total\ montly\ debt\ payments}{Total\ net\ monthly\ income}$$

Your total net monthly income is the income that actually reaches your household, such as your paycheck. This way, you can see how much of your take-home pay is going towards debt.

You want to keep your DTI below 30% or as low as possible. A DTI of less than 30% looks good to lenders and has a positive impact on your credit score. If you're having issues maintaining a low DTI, try stopping the use of credit altogether until you're able to get a better handle on your finances. If that isn't possible, focus on increasing your discretionary income (the money remaining after paying taxes and expenses). Widen the gap between income and expenses paid. We'll discuss credit and debt further later as we cover designing a debt reduction strategy.

Who uses the debt-to-income ratio? Well, any lender who is considering giving you a loan will take a look at your DTI to see how you are handling your current debt and your capability to handle more debt. They look at this in addition to your credit score.

What Your DTI Says About Your Financial Health
Think of DTI as a measure of breathing room.
- A **lower DTI** means a smaller portion of your income is tied up in debt. You have more flexibility, more financial stability, and more capacity to handle emergencies or new expenses.
- A **higher DTI** means more of your income is already spoken for, leaving you with less cushion and more vulnerability to financial stress.

How Lenders Interpret Your DTI
Potential lenders view your DTI as a direct indicator of risk:

1. Ability to Repay
The lower your DTI, the more confident a lender feels that you can take on new debt and still comfortably

make payments on your loans on time consistently.

A high DTI signals that you may be stretched thin and could struggle to manage additional monthly obligations.

2. Financial Reliability

Lenders want borrowers with a track record of manageable and structured finances. A reasonable DTI reflects not just ability, but financial **behavior.** It shows you don't take on more debt than your income can realistically support.

3. Lending Terms You'll Receive

Your DTI affects:
- Whether you get approved
- Your interest rate
- Your credit limits
- The size of the loan you qualify for

A strong DTI can unlock better rates and more favorable terms. A high DTI can result in denials or require you to have a co-signer or pay a higher rate.

DTI Benchmarks Lenders Use

While exact thresholds vary by lender and loan type, the general guidelines are:
- **Below 36%:** Excellent. Lenders see this as low risk.
- **36%–43%:** Acceptable. Many mortgage lenders consider this the maximum qualifying range.

- **Above 43%:** High risk. Approval becomes more difficult.
- **Above 50%:** Very high risk. Most lenders will decline applications until debt is reduced.

Bottom Line

Your debt-to-income ratio tells lenders two critical things:

1. Can you afford more debt?
2. How likely are you to repay it on time?

Improving your DTI by reducing debt, increasing income, or both, strengthens your financial foundation and opens the door to better financial opportunities.

Credit Score

A credit score is a number that represents your creditworthiness, or in other words, how likely you are to repay a loan. It's based on several factors that we'll go over in step five: The Leveraging Credit Blueprint.

Your credit score is a financial status indicator that you've likely heard a lot about. There are a ton of commercials and other advertising urging you to increase your credit score. You're likely aware that you need a great credit score for many things. There are also a lot of credit repair companies offering solutions to fix your credit report and increase your credit score, especially for those who have complicated errors and delinquencies on their credit report.

A credit score is the financial status indicator that most lenders and other businesses use to determine how well you can handle your money and credit.

Years ago, you had to pay to obtain your credit score. You could get your credit report (the history of your credit use) for free, but you would have to pay to get your score. However, these days you can get your credit score for free through credit monitoring sites. Even some credit card companies will provide your score for free.

Get your credit score to see your creditworthiness. The higher the score, the better. While there are multiple formulas to calculate a credit score, FICO is the most common. We'll go into more depth in section five: The Leveraging Credit Blueprint. For now, just look up your score so you can use it in determining your baseline financial fitness.

Generally speaking, a score of 580 or higher is fair to excellent. This is looked upon more favorably by lenders. We'll go deeper in step five.

Financial Status
Once you have determined your WISE Score, net worth, debt-to-income ratio, and your credit score, you'll have a comprehensive snapshot of your current financial status as well as your current wealth.

This picture of your current financial status is the basis for determining your financial goals. This is key to moving from where you are to where you desire to be. You'll learn about designing financial goals in step two.

Chapter 2: Your Financial Plan

Keeping your financial information organized is another key element of a comprehensive money management system. In this chapter, we will discuss how to organize your financial data to successfully achieve your financial goals.

Master File
Create a master file that contains a list of the financial accounts in your financial system and their purpose. Create a table with columns for:
- the type of account,
- the purpose of the account,
- the goal dollar amount, and
- the monthly contributions as necessary.

Include all your checking accounts, savings accounts, investment accounts, insurance information, etc. Of course, keep this in a secure place and encrypted so others don't have access to your information.

Most websites and software use a username, password, and security questions combination for access. You can keep a physical or digital password book or use password management software to keep track of your passwords and security questions.

If you do use a physical password book, make sure that you keep that notebook in a very secure location so that people don't happen upon all your login information, the figurative keys to the kingdom.

Filing Financial Documents

The next item in your organization system is a filing system on your computer and a physical filing system for your paper financial documents, such as bills, insurance, and tax documents received via mail.

For the digital filing system, start with an overall folder labeled 'financial documents' or 'financial system,' something to that effect. Within that folder, create sub-folders for each household bill or budget category. For example, have folders for mortgage/rent, gas and electric, phone bill, etc.

Within each bill or budget category folder, include the bill statement and the payment receipt. Most of us pay bills online these days, so use a printout or PDF of the confirmation page as a receipt. These can be used in case anything goes wrong. For example, the company says they didn't receive your payment. You will be able to provide the payment confirmation number and a copy of the confirmation page as proof that you paid the bill, and not just paid it, but paid on time. For bills that are automated, save the "your bill is paid" confirmation email as a PDF so you can save that in your files.

Create a second tabbed folder for tax documents. Within this folder, create subfolders for each tax year. Within each subfolder, place the documents you will need to file your taxes for that year. If you've donated to charities, then include a copy of the acknowledgement and estimated monetary value sheet in the folder.

Keep a copy of your W-2 from your employer. Other documents that you may need include:

- any 1099 forms,
- canceled checks or printouts of confirmation numbers from estimated tax payments made,
- investment end-of-year statements that show interest income, dividend income, and income from sales,
- a report of rental property income,
- a profit and loss report of your side hustle income
- any other documents that show income or benefits received that you may need to report on your taxes, e.g., 1099.
- any other document that supports a tax credit or deduction, e.g., daycare payment receipts

For your physical filing system, use the same breakdown. Have folders for each bill. Keep track of confirmation numbers after making a payment. Write the confirmation number on the corresponding paper bill to reduce paper usage and make it easier.

Again, make sure your digital and physical financial documents are in a secure location. For your digital filing system, use some level of device or password security, such as password protecting the computer and creating a separate visitor or guest account for others to use if you allow other people to use your computer. You may also want to encrypt the actual financial folder.

Once you're using your financial organization system, the paperwork and the files can really add up. So, you may be wondering how you know when you can shred and trash them. The length of time you need to store a document depends on the type of document and why it's needed. For example, save tax-related documents in case you need to amend your tax return or if you get audited. If you made a mistake or discovered there was a tax break you could have claimed, then you may need to amend your tax return.

Keep tax documents for at least three years. The IRS can audit you for up to three years after filing a tax return. You also have three years after your filing date or two years after paying the tax to claim a refund or credit. Under certain conditions, the IRS can audit you for up to six years. If you underreported your income by more than 25% then the IRS has six years to file an audit. If there is a possibility that you didn't add all income to a 1040 form or didn't report some income, then keep your documents for at least six years.

If you didn't file a tax return, then keep documents that explain why. For example, if your income was below the filing limit or you had no taxable income.

Other Types of Documents
There are other documents you should file besides tax documents. Here is how long you should keep financial documents.

1) Receipts:
You can throw out receipts after you make sure the purchases have cleared in your bank or credit card statement and you've accounted for the expenses in your expenses tracking system. Receipts for major purchases such as appliances, home repairs, contractors, etc., should be kept:
- until any warranties have expired,
- as evidence for taxes as necessary, and
- if they would be needed in rent or home insurance claims.

2) Credit card and bank statements:
Review your statements for accuracy and then file them in the appropriate folder. After one year, you can shred and trash them. If they contain something you need for taxes, then put them with the tax documents.

3) Investment statements:
File monthly statements for the entire year. When the annual summary statement arrives, if it reflects all your activity, you can shred the *monthly* statements for that year. Save the *annual* statement since you still have the investments.

4) Real estate records:
Keep everything. File purchasing documents and any documents related to home improvements or repair until seven years after selling the property.

The filing system only works if you actually use it. It can be easy to set monthly statements aside or read the email and never save the statement. Decide on a filing schedule and stick to it. For paper statements, either handle them when they come in and file them or keep them in a designated place and pick a day and time every month that you can then go through and file your financial documents.

When it's time to throw out documents, it is best to shred them. Don't trash documents that have your account numbers or personal identification information on them. Either invest in a small shredder or rip them up by hand. Ripping up by hand was my method for a long time. If you're shredding by hand, make sure to tear the paper into tiny pieces and mix them with regular stinky trash. Hey, you can't be too careful. If someone is going to try to steal your identity or information, then make them work really hard for it. A shredder also comes in handy for things like credit cards, but scissors work well for that too.

Step 2: The Power of Mindset Formula

Chapter 3: Money Ideology

Money is a tool. How you use that tool depends on your money ideology. Your **money ideology** is your viewpoint regarding having money, earning it, and spending it. It's developed from your experiences and from what you're taught about finances.

Money is just a tool made of paper and metal, but it's tied to very emotional experiences and desires. You're not working on bettering your finances just for the money. A certain level of money is required for financial security, to afford the things you want to buy, and to afford the travel you desire. The things that you can buy with money are the incentive. The places you will be able to go provide motivation. The potential to decrease financial stress and being prepared to handle a future emergency or large expense is a powerful reason for change.

To become a master wealth builder, you have to determine and understand your money ideology. Knowing your money ideology will help you work with yourself to better your finances. For example, we only truly need a few things to survive. We need food, water, shelter, and I'll add socializing. Everything else, you can survive without having it, but you **want it**. The other things you purchase make life more comfortable and enjoyable.

Your inner dialogue and reasoning when spending money, in other words, how you go about getting those "other things," corresponds with your money ideology.

For example, are you only buying new cars, regardless of your current resources and cash flow? Or do you consider buying used cars too? Do you automatically take advantage of most sales, or do you check your budget first?

I've found there are three main money mindsets related to spending.

1) Sense of entitlement
The first money mindset is the **sense of entitlement mindset**. This is when a person uses the "I deserve it" rationale to justify purchasing luxury items rather than items they can afford. Or simply purchasing more than they can afford.

A person with a sense of entitlement money mindset will use the phrase "I deserve it" or an iteration of this phrase to justify purchases. I'm not saying that it's just an excuse, and they don't deserve it. Not at all. Deserving or not is a moot point. It's the logic or mindset that I'm pointing out. It doesn't matter whether you explain why you feel you deserve it or what the item costs.

Buying a $1 slushie by saying "I deserve it" or buying a $200 dress by saying "I deserve it" is the same. It is the sense of entitlement mindset causing you to spend when you don't need the item and haven't made sure you can afford it.

There is nothing wrong with splurging once in a while, provided it's within your means. However, don't use the sense of entitlement as an excuse to alter your lifestyle to something that you can't afford. Recognize when you are having this dialogue with yourself. As soon as you think I deserve something, follow it up with the question, "But can I afford it right now?"

There's probably no doubt that you deserve whatever the item is, but if you save up to buy it, then you won't disrupt or sacrifice something else to get it. You deserve it, or you want it. Either is ok, just be able to buy it without creating a financial deficit or sacrificing something important. How do you do that? You price the item and save up to get it. Don't try to keep up with the Joneses. Try to keep money in your wallet.

2) Immediate Gratification

The second money mindset is the **immediate gratification mindset**. A person with this mindset is more likely to make impulsive purchases rather than researching an item before making a purchase. When shopping or simply out and about, they see something, get excited, and make a purchase. They want it or can think of a great or cool way to use it, so they buy it. They reason something to the effect of: if I already know how I'm going to use it, then I need it, so it's ok, a great find actually.

Well, while it may be a great find, it's also an impulse buy done for immediate gratification. You saw something, you wanted it, and you bought it. However, ask yourself if you really went through all the scenarios of how you could and would use it. If so, would you decide that it's a want or a need? Or if you left the store without it and thought about it for a few days, would you miss it or need to go back and purchase it? If it's a want or you wouldn't miss it, then just leave it if you can't afford it. You could put the money towards something else, even better!

There is definitely something to be said for waiting and deferring gratification. You can save for the purchase instead, or wait for the item to go on sale. When you buy an item impulsively, you often end up paying more for it. Before you make a purchase, ask yourself questions to determine if the item is a need or a want and if you can afford it.

Train yourself to institute a waiting period where you really consider the item that you're excited about. Chances are, if you wait, you'll realize or decide that you really do not need it. Often, if it's something exciting, it's a want, not a need, unfortunately.

3) Emotional Purchasing

The third money mindset is the **emotional purchasing mindset**. This can run the gamut of emotions, from extreme happiness to extreme sadness. Most people are familiar with the term "retail therapy." People often resort to retail therapy when something in life or the day is not going as planned, and they need a pick-me-up, so they turn to shopping. Why? For some, going shopping is generally fun. They're scouting merchandise, looking for the perfect skirt, pants, shirt, shoes, etc. It's a whole adventure, and when it's successful, they feel great! They found what they wanted or even found something they didn't need, but it was such a bargain! There was no way they could leave it there! Does that sound familiar?

Usually, when people hear the term retail therapy, it is associated with emotions on the sadness or upset end of the emotional spectrum. Unfortunately, it's also a very expensive habit. There are going to be many times when things aren't going right, and you need a pick-me-up. Don't go to the store! Find an alternative activity that can center you and help you regain your positivity. I call it a de-stress activity. It's different for all of us. Some people like to get lost in a good book or a good movie, while others prefer going for a walk or dancing. Whatever activity makes you feel good and is good for you, find it and do it when you're upset or sad. Finding a positive de-stress activity will prevent you from running to the store for a pick-me-up, which can severely deflate your wallet.

What many people don't know or consider is that emotional purchasing also occurs at the other end of the emotional spectrum, when you're happy or excited. Some people, when they are happy or excited after a big accomplishment or event, want to keep the good times rolling and will head to the store. Don't go to the store!

Reminisce about what is making you happy and bask in it. Heading to the store and spending money when you can't afford it will only make you frown later. Another emotional reason people tend to spend is that an object or a happy memory evokes a positive feeling. "Remember when we used to… (fill in the blank)." Bask in the memory and the feeling, but try not to run out and buy the item to recreate it. You'll be happy about the money still in your wallet.

Take the time out to determine which money mindset you have. Don't skip this, as you want to keep your money mindset in mind when you structure your money strategy later. For the next couple of weeks, when you go out shopping, be very conscious of the dialogue you have with yourself. What is your reason for purchasing an item? Be honest with yourself. Don't just say, "Well, I needed it." Did you really need that specific item? Was it a genuine need? Was it really in your budget?

For example, say you need an outfit for an upcoming event. Your budget is $50. You go shopping and find the perfect outfit. It fits you well, you look amazing. You check the price tag and see that this outfit costs $200. You think well, I need it. It will help me accomplish my goal for the event, and dang it, I deserve it.

Hmm, in this scenario, to stay on track with spending, the person likely could have come up with a similar outfit that stayed under $50. Are you sure that absolutely nothing in your closet would have worked? Was there nothing that could have been purchased for less than $50 and combined with something in your closet that would have accomplished the same goal? Was it really a need? We know the answer to that is no. It's a want.

For the next couple of weeks, as you go shopping, think about the real reason that you're buying something. No matter how small the item is, reason it out prior to the purchase. You'll narrow down on your money mindset very quickly. You may be a mix of more than one, and that's ok too.

Working with Your Money Mindset
Once you're aware of which spending money mindset you have, you can work with yourself to structure a money strategy that will work best for you. You'll be able to exercise discipline and strengthen willpower once you're clear on what is causing you to oppose them. You'll start to recognize when you're using that logic to engage in behavior and spending habits that are detrimental to your financial success.

When in a store, it can be hard to remember why you shouldn't purchase something. Take a visual reminder with you. Write a note and wrap it around your credit and debit cards. Set your phone's wallpaper to something that reminds you of your goals.

Implement these changes and give yourself time to change your habits. It will take time to shift to a wealthy mindset and develop wealthy habits.

Chapter 4: Developing a Wealthy Mindset

In this chapter, we will discuss how to cultivate a wealthy mindset. We'll cover what it means to have a wealthy mindset, how it will show up in your life, and how to implement it through wealthy habits.

A wealthy mindset is crucial to financial success. Even if it sounds corny or silly to you, recognize that building wealth starts with the decision and belief that you can do so. You have to believe it is possible for YOU.

When you believe you can accomplish a task or a goal, you start taking action to make your belief or vision a reality. Even when there is a setback, you view it as temporary, and you plot how to get around the obstacle. You ponder **how** you can overcome challenges to achieve your goal, versus wondering **if** you can do it. Why? Because you have the *belief* you can do it, or in other words, you have already made the decision that you will achieve it.

Alright, I still haven't said exactly what it means to have a wealthy mindset or how to develop one. Here are six easy steps to follow and cultivate your wealthy mindset.

1) Decide to be wealthy.
We already talked about this step above. You need the belief that you can build wealth and that you will accomplish this goal. Make the decision that YOU can and will be wealthy, then stick to it no matter what obstacles arise. There's a solution to every challenge.

2) Be rich, don't just look rich.

Next step, get committed to not just looking rich. You want to actually have money in the bank with commas and trailing zeros, not just *look* like you have a lot of money using societal stereotypes.

Don't spend money on buying things you can't afford to impress people and then be worried about how you're going to pay your bills. The people that you're trying to impress are not paying your bills. They're not the ones who will be stressed out, wondering if there's enough money to pay all the expenses needed to survive, take care of their family, and invest.

If you manage your money well and live below your means (spending what you can afford), then you can achieve financial goals with your salary. I know it may feel like you need a large multi-six-figure salary and maybe a winning lottery ticket to be wealthy or properly prepare for retirement, but that just isn't true. You don't need to have a huge salary to become a millionaire, but you do need wealthy habits and discretionary income. The more discretionary income, the better.

Save and invest over time to build wealth. The more time you have to save and invest continuously, the more likely it is that you will become a millionaire on an average American salary. However, establishing multiple income streams will accelerate wealth building. Of course, the more money you have to put to work building wealth, the faster you will be able to reach your financial goals.

This is why it's so important not to waste money on looking rich, but to put your money towards actually becoming rich. Hmm, well, not just rich, but wealthy.

3) Change what you consume.
Does the content you watch, listen to, or read help you achieve your goals, or do they just fill time? Some things we consume for fun, entertainment, and laughs. However, you also need to consume content that will enlighten you and help you with your goals. Review the music, podcasts, shows, movies, books, blogs, etc. that you consume regularly. Ask yourself, what purpose do they serve?

To create and sustain a wealthy mindset, change what you consume. Ok, so what does that mean? Well, consider how you consume news and entertainment. You likely watch TV and videos online. You listen to music and radio programs. You read books, blogs, and websites.

What happens if you change the material you consume through all these mediums? Instead of watching a sitcom or entertaining YouTube videos, you watch a program about finances or investing. Instead of listening to music on your commute to work or as you do chores, you listen to a podcast about finance, advancing your career, or making more money. Instead of reading entertainment or news articles, switch to or include blogs about finance, career development, and making more money.

Effortlessly extend your learning by switching what you consume. This will help you develop a wealth mindset and shift your habits.

4) Do more financial planning.
Increase the amount of time spent on financial planning and designing strategies to make more money. Plan for your success. I want you to be honest with yourself. Think about the amount of time you spend on your finances per month. If all you do is review your budget, then there is a problem.

Yes, it is important to review your budget, but it's also really important to review your personal money strategy and the overall plan to build wealth. Financial planning is not a "set it and forget it" activity. Each month, analyze your budget and determine which actions are needed to make progress toward your financial goals.

Review your money strategy and make sure you're taking actions that will
- lower your tax burden,
- prepare for large upcoming expenses such as a vacation or paying for a child's higher education, and

- free up more money to put towards actions that increase your net worth, such as paying off high-interest debt, saving, and buying assets.

These three tasks will help optimize your cash flow and increase your discretionary income. With more discretionary income, determine how you can invest more money in retirement and non-retirement investment accounts.

I remember reading in The Millionaire Next Door that the average person will spend 2-3 hours on financial planning per month. The average millionaire will spend 20-30 hours on financial planning. The average millionaire spends 10x more hours per month planning and analyzing how they can optimize cash flow and make more money than the average person. Change what you consume and act on what you learn.

5) Don't wing it.
Make and follow a plan and engage in wealthy habits. The next step for your wealthy mindset is to make and follow a plan. Don't wing it. You're already reading this book, which will help you to formulate a plan and create wealthy habits ... if you act on what you learn. This will be crucial to your financial success. I've heard people say, "I don't believe in planning. I just look for opportunities." At that point, I always have owl eyes (open my eyes wide). I must have a plan, especially when it comes to finances.

I agree that identifying opportunities is very important. However, you also need at least a general plan on how you will achieve your goals. This will allow you to really keep an eye out for the right opportunities as well as create opportunities that will allow you to reach your goals.

Make a financial plan. Continue to optimize it as you learn more and get new opportunities. Winging it is not an option. Your goals are too important.

6) Realize it won't be quick; slow and steady wins.

The last, but in no way least, step to create and sustain your wealthy mindset is to realize and accept that it's not a quick road to wealth. Slow and steady is what will get you there. You will need to maintain these wealthy habits day in and day out, every month, every year.

That's not to say you can't have fun or splurge once in a while. You surely can, but with wealthy habits, you'll have the money to do so and won't rack up any new debt or feel guilty for indulging. You'll be able to have luxury in frugal living because you'll be money savvy.

Chapter 5: Financial Goals Planning

In this chapter, we'll discuss how to set primary and secondary financial goals and design a plan to achieve them. We'll also discuss how to break down goals into manageable tasks and sub-goals for success.

You will always have financial goals. Your financial journey is lifelong because your financial status is fluid, and there is always a new goal. As a result, your journey is filled with intermediate milestones. These milestones are financial goals that stair-step to reach your ultimate, primary, and secondary financial goals. To maintain the goals achieved and progress to the next goal, you have to continue wealthy habits.

You may have heard the terms short-term and long-term goals. However, those are actually sub-goals. You have one primary financial goal and many sub-goals or milestones beneath it that will help you achieve it. You continue or move through the goals until you accomplish your primary goal.

For example, say your ultimate financial goal is to achieve financial freedom. Or your primary financial goal is to establish financial security by preparing for retirement and building wealth. Or perhaps your primary financial goal is to leave a legacy of wealth for your family and your community. To achieve your primary goal, you need sub-goals such as a fully funded emergency fund, being debt-free, maxing out your 401(k) each year, and buying non-retirement assets.

This is why your money strategy is the plan to achieve these goals and accomplish your ultimate goal.

To achieve the secondary goals, you'll also have many sub-goals for each. Different goals will take different lengths of time to accomplish. That is where the terms short-term and long-term goals come into play. However, those terms can be very broad and open to too much interpretation, especially if you're struggling with your goals. Instead of labeling goals short-term or long-term, split them into 30-day, 90-day, 6 months, 1 year, and 5 years. Those categories are very clear about the time to completion and are a better way to help you stay on track and in action.

S.M.A.R.T. Goals

Remember: When designing financial goals, review your current financial situation and consider the tasks needed to reach your final destination. This will help you determine your sub-goals, or in other words, secondary goals and milestones.

Clearly define your goals so it's obvious when they have been achieved. There is a great acronym to help you. The acronym is S.M.A.R.T. It stands for specific, measurable, attainable, realistic, and time-sensitive. Make sure that your goal contains all of these elements. Many times, when people state a goal, it's not a real goal at all. It's a wish or vague statement of a desire. For example, I'm going to save more money. This statement is way too vague. It is not motivating and doesn't give you any actionable steps. Let's revise it using the S.M.A.R.T. acronym.

Let's say, from your budget, you know you have $100 to save every month. The goal is to save $100 per month for six months. Is it specific? Yes, I know exactly what action to take. Is it measurable? Yes, I have an actual dollar amount and know that at the end I should have $600. Is it attainable? Yes, I know I can add $100 per month to my savings. Is it realistic? Yep, I already ran the numbers in my budget. Is it time-sensitive? Yes, I'm going to complete this goal in six months.

You see how that's much different than just saying I want to save more? Reviewing your finances and creating concrete S.M.A.R.T. goals will be crucial for your financial success.

Common Financial Goals

If you're struggling with creating goals, start with this list. These form the foundation for good financial goals. Remember to convert them into S.M.A.R.T. goals that apply to your situation.

- Establish an emergency fund
- Eliminate credit card debt
- Pay off student loans
- Pay off a car loan
- Pay off the mortgage
- Take a vacation once or twice a year
- Save for retirement
- Acquire or grow investments

Design Your Financial Goals

Review the numbers and financial status indicators you calculated in Chapter One. The following exercise will help you think about your financial situation and determine which goals you need. Close your eyes, take a deep breath, and consider your current financial situation. How would you describe it? Think about when you pay bills. How do you feel? Are you anxious? Stressed? Is it just routine? Would you be able to handle a financial emergency? How would you feel if you unexpectedly had to put out a large sum of money? Could you do it? Would you have money readily available?

Take a moment to do this thinking exercise and write down the answers to the above questions. After, answer "How do you feel about your current money situation?"

Once you understand your current financial situation, consider where you want to be with your money. What does financial success or financial freedom look like for you? Who is with you? Where are you? When you achieve financial freedom, how do you feel? Now, would you be able to handle a financial emergency? How would you feel if you unexpectedly had to pay a large sum of money? Could you do it, and would you have the funds?

Take a moment to answer the above questions. The answers to these questions will help you determine which goals you need to achieve your ideal version of financial freedom.

Here's some additional guidance. **If you don't have any savings, an emergency fund should be a top priority.** It will take a while to complete your emergency fund, but aim to have at least $1,000 as an intermediate step. Currently, the cost of an average emergency is $500 or less, e.g., replacing car tires or replacing a water heater. Therefore, getting at least $1,000 in your emergency fund should allow you to handle the average emergency. If you need to shift your focus to a different financial goal, such as paying down consumer debt, before completing your emergency fund, you know you won't suffer a complete financial disaster.

If you have any illnesses, potential upcoming medical bills, or even the need for over-the-counter medicine, then increase the intermediary emergency fund amount to $2,000. **If your income is inconsistent** or relies on something like having a tenant in a rental property, then up that bare minimum emergency fund to three months' worth of bills. If there is something unique to your life that, if it needed to be replaced or repaired, would be an emergency for you, then make sure to include the cost of that item when determining the amount to have in your emergency fund.

If you have credit card debt, that should be the next priority after establishing the bare minimum emergency fund. Credit card interest rates range from around 6% to over 36%. The average interest rate is around 22%. At such rates, your debt will grow faster than your wealth. Therefore, prioritize paying off high-interest debt, such as credit card debt.

For each goal, write the tasks you need to complete to accomplish the goal. These become your sub-goals. This will also help you to create a task list to achieve your goals. Write your primary financial goal and at least two secondary financial goals for the year, and the goals to be completed in five years. Remember the breakdown from before: 30 days, 60 days, 90 days, 6 months, 1 year, and 5 years.

It's crucial to write your goals down. Make them concrete and hold yourself accountable.

Prioritize Your Goals

Once you write down your goals, to make the deadlines make sense, you have to prioritize them. Determine what order to work on the goals to achieve financial freedom. I can be "Team Too Much," envisioning achieving all my goals at once. I know, I set myself up sometimes. It's easy to dream big. Perhaps you're envisioning buying a home, growing your savings, starting a business, taking multiple vacations, or traveling the world. You may want them all right now. However, the truth is, trying to do everything at once often leaves us overwhelmed and farther from our goals. We only have so much time, energy, and money to put towards achieving our goals.

We have to prioritize what matters most. I often remind myself and have planning sessions to prioritize and revise my strategy as needed. Here's a simple process to set clear, achievable goals:

1) Start with your "why."
Answer the following questions. Why did you make the goal? Why is it important for you to achieve it? What will make the most significant impact on your life? What is the largest motivator for your primary goal? What will bring you the most joy?

2) Assess your current situation and resources.
You assessed your current financial situation in Chapter One. Take that assessment and answer … what's realistic and will allow the most progress given your time, money, and energy?

3) Focus on the top three.
Narrow your goals to the three that align with your priorities and will move you closer to your vision of financial freedom.

Once you've outlined your goals, it's time to create a plan to achieve them. A critical step is understanding your financial picture. This is why that was the first thing you had to do. If you skipped the assessment, go back to clarify your true financial situation. Be honest with yourself about your situation. This is key to designing a strategy to achieve your goals. For example, you'll need a different strategy if you're aiming to catch up on household bills vs. get rid of a lot of debt vs. focus on aggressively saving vs. getting laser focused on investing, etc.

Step 3: The Elevate Your Money Formula

Chapter 6: Designing a Realistic Budget

Now that you have an excellent grasp on your current financial situation, your version of financial freedom, and the financial goals you need to accomplish to achieve it … you're ready to start designing your money strategy. Your comprehensive money strategy includes

- a budget, aka spending plan,
- a savings strategy,
- a debt elimination strategy, and
- an investment strategy.

In this chapter, we will discuss creating a W.I.S.E. budget. One of the major reasons people don't stick to budgets is that they're too tedious, or in other words, time-consuming and restrictive from the start. We're going to discuss how to design a realistic budget. This is a budget that meets you where you are and guides you to where you need to be to reach your financial goals. It corresponds with your goals.

If you're the type of person who, when you hear the word budget, screw up your face and think "ugh, here we go," first off, kudos for moving forward with reading this chapter. Give yourself a mini-celebration for getting out of your own way and for being dedicated to making progress with your finances.

To design your budget, first determine your current spending habits. Gather your bank statements and receipts from the past 30 days; get the past 60 days if you can. Take out a sheet of paper, Microsoft Excel, or

Word. Create four columns. Label them categories, amount, type, and percent of spending.

Organize Expenses
Use the bank statements. Perform the following tasks to gain clarity on your spending.

1) Determine budget categories based on where you spent money. Some common categories are home (rent or mortgage), utilities (gas and electric), food (groceries and restaurants), entertainment, clothes, personal care, and home supplies.

2) Next, look at spending for the past 30 days only and place the individual transactions into the categories you just created.

3) Calculate the amount spent in each category. This is the amount you spend in each category per month.

4) Add all the numbers in the amounts column, and that is your total spending in one month.

5) In the column labeled type, write if it is a need or a want. A need is something that ensures your survival. A want is something you could do without and still survive.

6) In the last column, titled percent of spending, calculate the percent of spending for each category.

Use this formula:

$$\% \, Spending = (\frac{Total \, category \, spending}{Total \, Budget})*100$$

Did you just say wow? I know; sometimes the numbers can be very shocking. A budget shows how much money you are spending in total and how much money you are spending in specific categories. It reveals where the majority of your money goes and where there are potential money leaks. This gives you an idea of your problem areas or categories and the areas where you're doing really well, spending within your means.

Congrats, you just made a .... budget! No, it's not the final product, but it's a necessary intermediate step. Congratulate yourself on the categories where you're doing really well, and cut yourself some slack in the areas where you aren't. You're a success rebel, so you're going to make shifts to fix those.

Sometimes your bank offers a tool that can do the above exercise for you. If so, take advantage.

Let's keep going.

Paycheck Breakdown

Let's discuss how to distribute your income based on your budget and goals. This is important for determining how much money is truly coming into your household and for assessing your budget and spending. Don't worry, we'll get to revising the budget, but we need to do this first. If you have inconsistent or variable income, plan your budget and paycheck breakdown based on the average income over 12 months, or use the lowest amount you would receive in a single month.

There are three levels of income that you should know: gross income, take-home pay, and discretionary income. Your gross income is your income before taxes. Your real spending power is in your take-home pay, the amount you have after taxes. Discretionary income is the money left over after paying expenses such as rent or mortgage.

A general paycheck breakdown:
Gross income minus taxes equals **take-home pay.**

$$Gross\ income - Taxes = Take\ home\ pay$$

Take-home pay minus expenses equals **discretionary income.**

$$Take\ home\ pay - Expenses = Discretionary\ income$$

Consider the dollar amounts that correspond to each faction of your income: gross, take-home, and discretionary. Let's go over an example. Say your annual income is $50,000. This is your salary or gross income. This would break down to about $4,166 per month. However, your gross income isn't the amount of money that comes into your home. Let's say you live in Maryland so that we can account for other taxes such as sales tax, property tax, FICA, etc. With a $50,000 salary you would pay approximately $17,581 in taxes. So, your take-home pay would be approximately $32,419. This breaks down into about $2,701.58 per month. Taxes make a big difference.

Gross income = $50,000/year or $4,166/month
Taxes = $17,581/year or $1,468.08/month
Take-home pay = $32,419/year or $2,701.58/month

The discretionary income would then be calculated by subtracting the monthly expenses for the household.

Taxes are a big chunk of your income. In the example, it's about 28%. Yes, you only receive approximately 72% of your salary throughout the year, depending on your tax bracket and other expenses, such as insurance, that come out before you get your check. In reality, you may receive less than 72% of your gross income. This is why your budget is based on the money that comes into your household, and why you have to consider benefits and taxes when evaluating job salaries. That 72% or less has to take care of the household and be put to work building wealth.

When creating a budget or spending plan, use your take-home pay and discretionary income, as these are the funds you truly have available to pay bills, cover other expenses, and build wealth. This is the money that you'll use to achieve your financial goals month after month, year after year, to build your wealth. As the years go by, the dollar amount should increase.

Alright, once you're clear on the dollar amounts for your take-home pay and discretionary income, it's time to divide up the amounts in your budget. There are multiple ways to create a budget. Pick the method that works best for you:

- You can stick with it to create, maintain, and update your budget.
- It is clear to you what the next steps you need to take with your money are to live within your means.

Here are standard budgeting methods:

1) 50/30/20 Budget
This may be the most common budgeting technique. It states that 50 percent or less of your budget should be spent on needs, things that are required for survival. If you don't have access to needs, then you die. Another 30 percent or less of the budget should be spent on wants. These are nice-to-have items and those

necessary for societal activities. The last 20 percent or less of your budget is then saved to put towards financial goals.

Income → 50% needs, 30% wants, 20% savings

2) 80/20 Budget
For this budgeting method, save 20 percent of your income, then spend the rest a la carte without budgeting each line item. This one is rather tricky to make work, as it's easy to overspend on non-fixed expenses. If you have any trouble with overspending, then this is likely not the best method for you.

Income → 80% needs and wants, 20% savings

3) Calendar Budget
Put your expenses and income on an actual calendar for this budgeting method. The calendar allows you a visual representation of when money will come in and go out. For some people, spreadsheets can be overwhelming, and using a calendar is more intuitive and useful. I highly recommend using a calendar. I call it a money calendar, and even as a person who loves spreadsheets, I like having a visual representation of my cash flow for the month as well.

4) Zero-based Budget
With this budgeting method, your income minus money going out (expenses, savings, investing) equals zero every month. This means that you must account for

every dollar of income with your spending and savings. When I first heard someone say they zero out their budget every month, I thought it meant they spent everything. That is not the case; savings are included in the budget.

5) Paycheck Budget

With this method, the budget is based on each paycheck rather than a lump-sum amount for the month. If you're finding yourself running low on money or even sometimes running out of cash before your next paycheck, this method will be beneficial. You designate each expense or a portion of an expense to each paycheck. If you have more expenses than your paycheck covers, pick a few bills to change their due dates. You can call the company and ask for the due date to be changed to a date after you will have received your next paycheck. This way, you're sure that you have the money to cover everything due for each specific paycheck.

Not Sure Where to Start?

The 50/30/20 rule is a great starting point if you're unsure which method works best, as it clearly shows what is within your means. Combine it with the paycheck budgeting method and a cash balance forecast to maintain a clear picture of how your income and spending are expected to be distributed.

I know a lot of things fall into the want category. For wants, spend no more than 30% of your income on them, whether it's clothes, entertainment, socializing, home improvement projects, etc. The last 20% of your take-home pay should be spent on savings, such as building your emergency fund, saving for other financial goals and large expenses, or contributing to your retirement account.

When you're just getting started, you may not yet be able to follow the 50/30/20 budget rule. If your necessary expenses are more than 50% of your income, what do you do? Well, you have to have a roof over your head, and you need to eat, so pay your bills and look for ways to decrease your expenses as well as increase your income.

Overhaul your current expenses and get rid of anything that doesn't support your financial goals. This will help to get your total necessary expenses as close to 50% as possible. Cut out non-essential expenses, except one. Keep one thing that helps maintain mental health. Cut everything else. For example, do you have cable and all the streaming platforms? How much do you really watch them? Can cable or some of the platforms go?

Once you've decided on what can be released, then focus on reduction. For which expenses can you reduce the cost? Can you get a better rate on expenses that you have to keep? Call the companies and find out. If you're a good customer who pays on time, they have an incentive to keep you rather than spending thousands to acquire a new customer.

Revise the Initial Budget

Once you've decided which budgeting methods you will use to design your budget, take the initial budget you created at the beginning of this chapter and revise it. The initial budget shows you where you are currently spending your money. The purpose of the revision is to design a budget and shift your spending plan to stay within your means and maximize the money that flows to financial goals.

When you revise your budget using the steps below, you'll be able to clearly see where your money is going and where you can lower expenses. You can see which companies you should call to lower your rates and decrease your expenses.

You can create a budget for any length of time you choose, but the most common and usually most applicable are a monthly budget and an annual budget broken down by month. If you use the paycheck method, then use the length of time that corresponds to your paycheck schedule, e.g., bi-weekly or weekly.

Earlier, you listed all expenses and grouped them by category. Now group those categories into two broad categories: fixed vs. non-fixed/flexible. Secondly, next to each expense write need or want. This will allow you to clearly see and calculate the percentage of your budget spent on needs versus wants.

After analyzing your expenses, it's time to optimize your budget. Create a new budget with lower limits for the expenses or categories where you determined you can or need to decrease the expenses. Remove the expenses or categories that you determined you can do without completely. For example, if you realized you spent $500 on food just for yourself, that's a lot of food, and that category can be reduced. Look up ways to cut your grocery budget back to at least $200. The "extra" $300 that was going to food can then be redirected elsewhere, like paying down debt. Just remember to remain realistic about the budget, don't make it too restrictive. Don't slash all expenses at once, as that will be very hard to maintain, especially once temptation arises.

Budget Guide

If you're struggling to determine an acceptable percentage to spend on specific line items, use this as a guide.

Budget Category	Percent
Rent/mortgage	30
Utilities	10
Food	10
Transportation	10
Health	5
Debt	5
Personal	5
Entertainment	5
Saving	20

After creating a monthly budget, design an annual budget. Do not simply multiply your monthly budget numbers by 12. Show the budget for each month side by side, then total that line item for the entire year. An annual budget will allow you to plan for expenses outside your normal monthly budget in advance.

The expenses that only happen at certain times of the year, such as birthdays and holidays, quarterly expenses, or annual expenses, can be prepped for and spread across several months if necessary. No more scrambling at the last minute and using a credit card to cover the costs. You'll also have an overall view of the true dollar amount you're spending in certain categories.

Chapter 7: Sticking to Your Budget

We just discussed how to design your budget and when and how to optimize it for your financial goals. Now let's make sure you stick to the budget so that you can make more progress with your goals. In this chapter, we're going to go over tips and tricks to help you spend within your budget (live within your means) and stay motivated.

Making Better Buying Decisions

Before we get to the tricks about revising the budget, let's discuss living within your means. This has to do with your buying decisions, as well as your budget. How do you determine if something is affordable? Use these eight rules as a guide.

Affordability is often misunderstood. Many people define it as having enough money in their account at the moment of purchase, but true affordability is not about whether you can pay today. It is about whether the decision preserves your financial stability tomorrow. A purchase you can afford supports your life, goals, and peace of mind without creating future strain.

1) Cash Flow

The first test of affordability is cash flow. Before buying anything, your essential expenses (housing, utilities, food, transportation, insurance, and debt obligations) must already be covered by your income. The purchase should fit within a defined spending category rather than forcing you to shift money away from necessities. If buying something today means scrambling to cover bills next month, the purchase is not affordable, regardless of how much money you currently have.

2) Pay Yourself First

Equally important is the habit of paying yourself first. Savings, investing, and emergency preparedness should be treated as non-negotiable financial commitments, not "I will if I can at the end of the month". A purchase is affordable only when it does not require you to pause contributions to your emergency fund, retirement accounts, or other priority savings goals. When you trade long-term security for short-term gratification, the real cost of the purchase becomes far higher than its price tag.

3) Wiggle Room

Affordability also requires having wiggle room in the budget, room to breathe. After making a purchase, you should still be able to handle an unexpected expense without relying on debt. Maintaining an emergency fund for essential expenses is not just a best practice; it is a safeguard against turning regular life disruptions into financial crises. If one surprise bill would undo your progress, the timing of the purchase deserves reconsideration.

4) No High-Interest Debt

Debt is another critical signal. If a purchase requires carrying high-interest credit card balances or adds financial pressure to an already strained debt situation, it is not affordable. Interest quietly magnifies the cost of spending decisions, often long after the excitement of the purchase has faded. While some investments, such as education or business tools, may justify careful borrowing, everyday spending should not create long-term financial drag.

5) The 24-72 Hour Pause

Time can be one of the most powerful decision-making tools. For nonessential purchases, pausing for 24 to 72 hours allows emotions to settle and clarity to emerge. When a purchase still aligns with your plan after the pause, it is more likely to be intentional rather than impulsive. Financial stress often stems not from what we buy, but from how quickly we decide.

6) Future Stability

A meaningful affordability test also considers your future self. Every dollar spent today is a dollar not available for future goals. When evaluating a purchase, it is worth asking whether it supports the life you are intentionally building or quietly delays progress toward debt freedom, flexibility, or long-term security. Opportunity cost is invisible, but it is always present.

7) Your Income Proportion

Context matters as well. The same purchase can be reasonable for one person and reckless for another, depending on income, obligations, and overall financial health. Affordability is not about comparison. It is about proportionality. Spending decisions should make sense relative to your financial reality, not someone else's highlight reel.

8) One-Time vs. Lifestyle Cost
Finally, it is essential to distinguish between one-time costs and lifestyle commitments. Many purchases carry ongoing expenses, such as maintenance, subscriptions, insurance, and replacements, that extend far beyond the initial price. People often can afford the purchase itself but underestimate the financial responsibility that follows. True affordability accounts for the full lifecycle cost, not just the moment of sale.

In the end, you can afford something when it fits comfortably within your cash flow, protects your savings and emergency buffer, avoids unnecessary debt, and aligns with your long-term goals. When those conditions are not met, the most financially disciplined answer is rarely "never," but simply "not yet."

Revising the Budget
Also, to live within your means, your total expenses should be less than your income. If expenses exceed your income, or there's hardly any money left after subtracting expenses from your income (discretionary or net income), you need to decrease the limit for more budget categories or increase your income. However, I know spending less can be way easier than quickly increasing your income. Revise the budget until the net income is zero or a positive number.

The **first trick is to choose language that works for you**. Words have power as they can influence how you view something. If you hate the word budget, call it a spending plan or something similar. For many, the term budget often creates a negative feeling or anxiety. However, it doesn't have to be this way. Do not think of budgets as restrictions or as a reason to abstain from things you like to do or want to have. Think of a budget as simply a plan for your money. It says where the money should go.

The main purpose of the spending plan is to give you more control over your money and a roadmap to direct more of your cash flow toward your financial goals. To accomplish a goal or task efficiently, you have to create a plan or strategy for how it will be done. Your budget is a part of the overall money strategy.

One of the major reasons people are unable to adhere to a budget is that it is way too restrictive. Those budgets are almost always ineffective. Don't just start slashing every budget category, thinking that will free up and save more money. What usually happens is that a person sticks to this for a month or less and then gives up. Instead, start where you are. Get a handle on what you actually spend and where you spend it, as you did above. Revise that rudimentary budget to design a WISE budget.

As you shift how you're spending, maintaining that shift can be very difficult. Most people fall off track and then have to get back on target. The goal is to make it rare and potentially avoid it altogether. You can do this by removing yourself as a roadblock. The **second tip is to automate as much as possible.** If your discipline is what's causing you to veer from the budget, then automation will be a big help. You can schedule automatic payments for bills with the same dollar amount each month. For those fixed expenses that you laid out in the previous chapter, see how many of them can be automated.

You can also automate bills that you know you need to pay anyway, like the gas and electric bill. You can do this through your bank or on the company's website, where you would normally go to make an online payment. Check if they have an automatic payment option. If the online payment system offers automatic payment, go ahead and set it up.

What this allows you to do is free up your time and energy to focus on other things, like making more money and enjoying time with your family. Automation helps you cut down on the amount of time required to pay bills since you're not logging into each system to pay bills or write out checks for some things that you may currently be writing checks to pay. I know writing checks is rare these days, but checks are still used in some places. Automation means that no matter what is happening that month, no matter what sales are going on, you don't have to have extra discipline to resist and maintain good financial behavior.

With automation, you decrease the amount of discipline that's necessary to live within your means and stay on track with your spending plan by removing yourself from the process. Your savings bill will get paid, and any other bills that are automated.

Of course, if there is a real emergency and you need to pause your automatic payments, you can do so, but only in extreme situations. Avoid making a habit of canceling or pausing automatic payments to afford something you want. That would be actively sabotaging your financial success.

The **third tip is to use the envelope system**. This system works great for those who need to curb overspending. With the envelope system, you take out the amount of cash you need for line items in your budget, the ones that aren't automated, and place the specific amount of cash for each bill or budget category in a designated envelope that has the name on it. For example, if the budget for eating out is $100, you would write "eating out" on an envelope and place $100 inside. When the money is gone, then the money is gone. There is no opportunity to overspend unless you withdraw more money. If you use this system, you have to consciously decide to overspend and break your budget, thereby foregoing your financial goals.

The envelope system keeps people accountable for staying on track with their budget. It's also been proven that people spend less money when they use cash than when they use a debit or credit card.

You may not like carrying cash, especially large sums. In that case, there is something different to try. Instead of carrying around cash, open up a second checking account. Transfer the money needed to pay the non-automated bills from the first checking account to the second checking account. Some banks will allow you to create spending buckets where you can designate specific dollar amounts to different categories. For example, instead of a paper envelope, you would have a digital spending bucket labeled "eating out" and designate $100 to the bucket.

For this second checking account, you also want to avoid overdraft fees. To keep the effectiveness of the paper envelope system in digital form, do not have overdraft protection on this second checking account. Overdraft protection allows transactions that you do not have the money to cover to still go through and leave you with a negative balance. You don't want to allow that because that means you're overspending. Therefore, for this second checking account, call the bank or log in online and opt out of overdraft protection. This way, when the money is gone, you can't overspend.

With a digital envelope system, you won't have to worry about carrying around cash or adding another chore of making it to the bank to take out cash. You can simply use the second bank account. Remember to leave the debit card for the first checking account at home so you're not tempted to use it when you run out of cash in the second checking account.

The next tip, **tip four, is to use lists when shopping**. I know, you may have tried lists before, and you always forget the list. Or if you took a list with you, you forgot to use it. You find the crumpled lists at the bottom of a bag later, or only remember when you run across the app on your phone that holds the list. Well, the thing is, lists actually do help you stay on track. Let's figure out how to get them to work for you.

1) Use the home screen of your phone.
You can use a digital list app on your phone's home screen. There are numerous apps. Look in the app store for your device. Whether you have an Android, Apple, or Windows product, search for a list-making app. You can even search online for the best list-building app for your device. By using an app, when you have your phone, you have your list. These days, we rarely leave the house without a cell phone.

2) Set a reminder on your phone.
When you decide to shop, set a reminder on your phone to use your list. It will take a while to develop the habit, so stick with it. Eventually, when you go shopping, you'll think, "Do I have everything? Oh yeah, let me check the list." In the meantime, the reminder will help.

The next tip, **tip five, is to use a visual reminder**. You know the saying, out of sight, out of mind. It's so true. So how do you keep your financial goals top of mind? Create a vision board or simply a large list to post in a location where you will see it frequently.

A vision board is basically a collage of images that represent your goals. To make a vision board, ask yourself these questions:

- What am I passionate about?
- What is most important to me (e.g., family, financial security, etc.)?
- How does each one show up?
- What needs to change, e.g., being able to spend more time with family?
- What do I need to achieve these changes?
- What environment do I want to have?
- Who's with me?

Once you're clear on how your financial goals will show up and how you want them to impact your life, then find images that represent the answers to these questions. You can get and cut up old magazines, print out pictures, or create a digital vision board. For a digital vision board, make a collage in PowerPoint or a design program if you already have one. Then you'll have a digital vision board that you can take with you everywhere. Answering those questions and creating a vision board or list will give you clarity on how you want some of your goals to show up. Place the vision board where you can see it every day.

Do the same with the list. Put it up where you can see it.

The final tip, **tip six, is to use multiple copies of your visual reminder**. Make copies of your vision board or list to put in other places where you may need a reminder in the moment. For example, put your visual reminder as your computer wallpaper to inhibit frivolous online shopping. If you made a digital vision board, then it's super easy to place the vision board as your wallpaper or as the screensaver on your computer, phone, or other mobile device. You can be reminded several times a day of the importance of sticking to your budget to curb overspending and to remind you why you're saving and investing.

I know a vision board can be rather personal, so you may not want to share it or have it as your wallpaper, where anyone can see it. You can also write a note on your bank or credit card to serve as a reminder before you make a purchase. The note can contain a question such as "Does this help with my financial goals?" Or you can write one of the answers to your vision board prep questions. Write something that will make you remember your goals in the moment.

Now you have five tricks to stick to your new budget. Get creative and come up with more tricks that will work for you. Also, don't be discouraged if they don't seem to work right away. Remember, it takes a while to establish a habit. You may have heard that it takes something like

21 days, but that's not quite true. It can take 65 days or more to establish a habit. Stick with it, and you'll be successful. Don't beat yourself up too much for slip-ups. Figure out what made you slip up and come up with a solution so that particular thing won't cause you to slip up in the future. Do that for each slip-up, and they'll be less frequent. You got this, and your financial security is worth it.

Chapter 8: Tracking and Monitoring Your Budget

Now you have a budget you can stick to that will help you make great progress toward your goals. Yes! This is a great step. The next step to your financial success is actually using, tracking, and monitoring your budget. In this chapter, we're going to review some tips and tools to do just that, as well as how to analyze your budget.

Tracking Spending

To make the best use of your budget, you need to track the distribution of your income, in other words, your spending, saving, and investing. In the previous chapters, we went through tips to help you create a good budget and maintain its use. However, that is the plan. Your budget is a projection. In other words, it is what you expect and plan to do with your money. You also need to consider actual transactions. You need to track what you actually did with your money. You want to be able to answer: how well you did with the plan, whether your projections were realistic, and whether you met your expected amounts.

Tracking helps prevent overspending by showing you when you're getting off track, but it's a more reactive than a proactive measure.

Tracking Methods

There are many different ways to track how you spend your money. The best way for you depends on whether you want to be very hands-on or more hands-off. As a busy professional, I'm going to guess the latter, but I'll go over options that encompass both.

1) You can use something simple and hands-on, like an Excel spreadsheet. There are a few templates available on the resources page. Input your monthly budget. As time passes, add the transactions that correspond with each budget category. This will allow you to see the spend down for each category.

2) There are online software tracking apps. There are numerous options, some free and some paid. These are great because they allow you to be a little more hands-off. Most online software will allow you to link your bank and debt accounts so that your transactions are automatically updated. The amount spent in each budget category is automatically updated, so you can monitor how you're doing with your budget. If the software places it in the wrong category or as miscellaneous, it's very easy to correct.

Some software also come with a mobile app, which is great for quickly checking your budget on the go so you can make sure you have money in that budget category before spending. I know this is great for staying on track. Another great feature of budgeting software is that most programs allow you to add goals, track bill due dates, and monitor debt paydown. It's great to have a visual of how your projected spending plan, aka your budget, will affect and is affecting your goals.

When I first started creating budgets and monitoring my spending, I used to use an Excel spreadsheet. I did this for years, but as my time became more limited, that became too tedious and time-consuming, so I switched to using online software for tracking. I still monitor some things and design my budget in Excel, but I use software to monitor spending. Sometimes I still use a combination of both when planning or creating a project-specific budget. Figure out the best method for you.

Remember, more hands off does not mean set it and forget it. You still have to assess and analyze your budget each month. Also, maintain your CFO (chief financial officer) meetings to review the analysis and determine actions to sustain progress towards financial goals.

If you're considering budgeting software, the sheer number of options can make it confusing to determine which one you need. Well, use this process. To pick budgeting software that will work for you, write out the features that are a must for you. Think about

- How do you want the data portrayed?
    - Calendar form, tables, pie charts, line graphs, etc.
- Do you want the program to sync to your bank and debt accounts?
    - Some people get a little nervous about this, which is entirely understandable. There are options that allow entering transactions manually.
- Do you want to be able to add goals?
- Do you want to be able to see your debt accounts?

- Do you want to be able to monitor your investments?

You may need to use more than one software application. For example, some budgeting programs aren't great at tracking investments, so you may need a separate program. Some of the programs that are great for monitoring investments and net worth aren't really great with budgeting. Try out a few. See what really works for you.

Analyzing your budget.
As you look at and go through your budget, you will ask yourself a series of questions. These questions will ensure you're properly conducting a general analysis of your financial data. Enough to help you determine if you're on track and what you should do if you're not on track. There are questions for general budget analysis, the mid-month check, and the deep dive review.

General Analysis
During your general budget analysis, these are the questions you should answer as you review your actual expenses.

1) Did I overspend?
- In which budget categories did I overspend?
- How can I decrease the spending in this category?
- If I can't decrease this category, can I move money from a different budget category to this one?

2) Did I underspend?

- In which budget categories did I underspend?
- Should I decrease the amount for these categories?
- Is this a consistent pattern? If so, where should I put the overage instead?

3) In which categories did I not spend at all?

- Is this a consistent pattern?
- Should I get rid of this category?
- Do I expect to spend in this category later in the year? If so, create an estimate of the cost. Divide that amount by the number of months until you expect to spend the expense. Use that number as the new amount for that budget category. Start putting that amount of money aside in a savings account.

4) Are my total expenses less than my income? How much money was left over?

- After paying bills and saving, was there money left over? How much? Put this money towards your financial goals. If this becomes consistent, then revise the budget to add this amount to your debt payments, savings, or investments.

5) Am I sticking to my budgeting rules, e.g., the 50/30/20 rule?

- How close am I to the rule?
- Am I getting closer over time?

6) How is my cash flow?

- Am I able to cover upcoming expenses?

If you will have an issue covering upcoming expenses, consider changing your due dates. If all your bills are concentrated around one pay date, sometimes it can be difficult and takes extra discipline to save the second paycheck so the money is there and can be used in addition to the next paycheck. If this is you, then call the companies and move the due dates.

Also, revise the budget to reduce expenses as much as possible. You may need to get more uncomfortable.

Outside of reducing expenses, another option is to increase your monthly income through a raise, a job change, a second job, or a side hustle.

7) What percentage of my income did I save?

- Did I stay on target?
- How can I increase the amount that I'm saving?
- Remember, if you're not currently saving 20% or more, then you're working your way to 20%. Keep checking on your progress. If you can save more money, then that's money you can put towards financial goals.

Mid-month Analysis

Complete a budget analysis in the middle of the month. Even if you don't feel you need to do a mid-month check-up or are taking a more hands-off approach, at least do a mid-month check for three months after starting a new budget. During this time, you'll be doing a lot of optimizing and adjusting the budget to make it the best budget for you. The mid-month check will help you determine adjustments needed to stay on track. Also, definitely do a mid-month check when you know you've purchased items you weren't necessarily planning to buy. You know, like from that sale you caught or the spontaneous night out with friends.

When you do your mid-month check, ask yourself:

1) Were there extraordinary expenses for the month? Does the budget need to be adjusted?

2) Am I off track?
- What actions can I take now to get back on track with my spending plan?

A mid-month check is a really quick analysis, so you can adjust your actions or budget as necessary to stay on track with your spending and, therefore, your financial goals.

Deep Dive Analysis

Every six months, do a deep dive into your finances. In addition to the general analysis questions, you'll ask yourself three additional questions.

Ask yourself:

1) What is my current net worth?

- We've gone over how to calculate your net worth. Every six months, recalculate it and see what the change is.

- At the end of the year, calculate your net worth and see if there is a change. It should be getting closer to zero if it's currently negative. If you already have a positive net worth, it should be getting larger.

2) What is my new W.I.S.E. Financial Fitness Score?

- Re-calculate your W.I.S.E. Financial Fitness Score. This will show you how your overall financial status has changed. You'll be able to assess your progress.

3) What is my new debt-to-income ratio?

- Remember, we reviewed this formula in chapter one. See how much progress you're making, specifically with decreasing your debt. We'll review the debt elimination strategy later.

Tracking, analyzing, and comparing your spending to the budget gives you the data you need to live within your means and put more money towards wealth building.

Chapter 9: Frugal Not Cheap

Being frugal is not about being cheap or being a miser. My motto is luxury in frugal living. You can still enjoy the now while working on your financial fitness. Think of frugal as money savvy, not being cheap. In this chapter, we're going to discuss ways that you can decrease spending while still having fun.

Identifying Budget Categories to Target
Decreasing non-fixed expenses can have the most significant immediate impact on cash flow. Review your budget and determine which categories you will target to reduce total spending. Some excellent categories are entertainment, eating out/food, gifts, clothes, personal care, and travel. These are usually flexible and mostly considered wants, not needs. Categories like eating out and travel are typically large and can be reduced.

You can get as hardcore with frugality as you like. Some people look for deals and coupons, and that's it. Some people become minimalists, selling or giving away most of their possessions. I've heard some entrepreneurs speak of minimalism, giving away everything except what can fit in a suitcase, and traveling, working from anywhere. Some people choose to do things like split two-ply toilet paper to stretch dollars as far as possible.

You don't have to do such things if you don't want to do them. I surely did not. However, you can be conscious of the decisions that you make when spending in the budget categories you identified. Make sure you're being frugal, stretching your money as far as it can go.

Let's use the entertainment budget category as an example. We've all been there. A spontaneous night out or a pricey restaurant meal unexpectedly stretched our budgets, and we completely blew the spending plan. Creating a set of rules will help you adhere to the entertainment budget. For example, a rule such as "I will only go out twice for the month or until I use my allotted entertainment money." If you go out once and spend your entire entertainment budget, then you're done for the month. Remember, such cutbacks are only for a specific period of time until you can afford to do more if you want.

For this example, one could be creative with going out during this time. Instead of going out to eat at a restaurant, have a potluck and game night. Each person can make and bring a dish. Everyone helps clean up. Rotate who hosts the potlucks.

Another frugal fun activity ... instead of heading to the movie theater, have a home movie night. A plain wall or a projection screen and a projector will allow you to create a large screen. If you usually stream movies and shows on your laptop, which would be too small for everyone to crowd around, a projector works wonders, or an HDMI cable, so that you can hook the laptop up to the TV. If you have a smart TV, then you can stream a movie via a platform. You can talk as much and as loudly as you want. Or not at all if that's your thing. You can get snacks at the grocery store, which will be much cheaper.

There are numerous ways to have frugal fun. Get creative and remember that it is for a period of time. Keep yourself motivated during that time. At some point, you may start getting the feeling of "ugh, I can't do this. I'm just going to buy this (whatever product or service you're considering)." This money is usually pulled from money that would have gone to savings or investments. When you get that feeling, look at your vision board and your goals list. Ask yourself if the activity you want to do or the item you wish to buy is more important than the goals on your vision boards. Will spending outside your budget get you closer or farther from your goals?

Let's go through another example using the travel or vacation category. When a person wants to take a vacation but is low on funds or wants to do so for as little as possible, I advise taking a staycation. A staycation is when you vacation right in your hometown or from your house. Do the touristy things in your city that you never do because, well, you live there.

Treat the staycation like a real vacation. Don't check the mail or email. Close and lock the office door, or remove all work- or school-related items from your view. Stick them in a closet, a box, or cover them with a blanket or sheet if you have large items that may be difficult to move, such as a bookcase filled with textbooks. Out of sight, out of mind.

Use sites that offer discounts and deals to find discounts on activities in your area. Let people know you're on vacation, so they cannot call you about work or school-related items. If someone contacts you anyway, we all have that one friend, respond with something akin to "I'm on vacay, so I'll have to get back to you later. Bye."

A staycation lets more of your vacation budget go toward activities and experiences. Accommodation is handled. Food can be obtained cheaply. There are negligible travel expenses.

As you engage in frugal practices, you may be worried about how others will view your actions. You may be thinking, "What will my family and friends think?" Just be frank. You don't have to explain anything to anyone outside of your household, but if you're worried about what others will think, say what you're comfortable with sharing. You can even use general statements such as "Yeah, I'm trying to knock out this debt, so for a time I'm being really frugal." Or "yeah, I'm on a strict budget as I work on my credit score / debt / buying a home" or whatever you'd like to put at the end.

Remember your why and its importance. You don't want other people not understanding the necessary changes in your financial behavior to affect your ability to maintain good financial habits.

Step 4: The Money Management System

Chapter 10: Your Saving Strategy

We've discussed your financial goals, how to design a useful budget to meet those goals, and that you should work on saving 20% or more of your income. Now let's discuss exactly where that 20% should go to build wealth. You need a strategy for dividing and distributing your money to reach your financial goals. In this chapter, we will discuss how to create a strategy to save for different goals, such as a down payment on a home, buying a car, and funding higher education.

When you have multiple financial goals that involve saving money, it may feel like you have more goals than you have money to fund them. So, what's the best strategy for funding these goals? Well, even though you may want to, you can't do everything at once. You can't save for every goal at once. As simple as it sounds, you'll have to prioritize which to tackle first, or else it will take exponentially longer to achieve each goal. From your budget, you know how much money you can save every month. This is the money available to use. Go back to your priority list for your financial goals. Remember, you prioritized your goals.

There are a few formulas that can help you design your savings goals. Determine which formula is best to use by considering:

- If there is a set amount of time to reach your goals, e.g., saving for a spring break or summer vacation.

- If there is a set dollar amount that is needed to achieve the goal, e.g., saving to purchase a washer and dryer set

If the goal needs to be achieved in a set amount of time, determine how much money you need to set aside every month to reach that goal in the specified amount of time. If it is a specific dollar amount, determine, based on the amount of money you can set aside each month, how long it will take you to achieve the goal. Check out the formulas below.

Saving for an Emergency Fund:

Your emergency fund is an excellent example of a savings goal for a specific dollar amount. Let's say you want to build a nine-month emergency fund.

Monthly Total Expenses x 9 = Total Savings

$$Total\ Savings = (Monthly\ Total\ Expenses)\ x\ 9$$

An emergency fund is 6-12 months' worth of bills set aside in an easily accessible account. During an emergency, you need money that you can get your hands on quickly. Cash is the most liquid, i.e., easily accessible form. If you are an entrepreneur, save 12 months' worth of bills. You may have a higher risk, contractors or employees dependent on you, and may need to funnel some money into business operations if the business experiences financial hardship. The best amount to put in your emergency fund depends on your situation: your financial status, employment status, industry stability, and risk tolerance.

Saving for an Event:
If you have to save a certain amount of money by a specific date, then use the formula below.

Total cost / number of months remaining = Monthly Saving

$Monthly\ Saving\ Total$

$= (TotalCost) - (Number\ of\ Months\ Remaining)$

Whether you are going on vacation or need to attend or host an event, it should have its own budget. It's usually a large, extraordinary expense. Use this formula to determine how much money you need to save every month to afford the event. Of course, if it's something like a flexible vacation, then you can use a bit of algebra and base the formula on how much you're able to save per month instead of time remaining:

Number of months remaining = Total cost / Monthly saving

The new formula tells you how many months it would take to save the total amount of money needed for the vacation, or in other words, when you would be able to go on vacation.

High-Cost Item Fund:

Occasionally, you may need to buy expensive items, which requires you to save money before you're able to purchase them. You can use the formula to determine when you can buy such items.

Total Cost / Monthly Saving = Number of months until purchase

These savings formulas are a great way to make sure that you live within your means. When you have a specific goal with a timeframe and dollar amount, it can be easier to stay on track and use cash, not credit.

The more time you give yourself to save, the smaller the monthly contributions can be and still reach your savings goals.

Saving is an important money management skill. The money saved is needed to help with financial stability and will be used for other financial goals. While you can't save your way to wealth, saving is an important building block for building wealth.

Here are the steps to craft your savings strategy.

1) Create a separate savings account for the goal.
It can be linked to your checking account, but do not try to save money in the checking account used to pay household bills. It will be spent if you do. Research which institutions have the highest interest rates for savings

accounts and any other necessary features you want, e.g., number of withdrawals allowed.

2) Clarify the dollar amount.
Do research and create a budget for what you need to achieve your goal. This gives you an estimated dollar amount needed.

3) Determine how much of your savings will go towards the goal.
I know, I just talked about prioritizing your goals and tackling them one at a time if possible. However, sometimes it's inevitable, and you have to work towards more than one saving goal at once. For example, you might need to save up to fund a child's trip or tuition while continuing to save for a home or a home repair. It's understandable.

Keep track of which goal the savings are going towards and try not to split the money you're saving more than three ways. Most banks and apps let you create buckets for specific goals. I suggest keeping the savings in one FDIC-insured bank account (guaranteed up to $250,000) and using buckets so the interest compounds on a larger amount rather than having multiple savings accounts for each goal.

4) Save the money.
Every month, put aside the right amount of money in the specified savings account. Be consistent and keep up with contributions.

5) Goal achieved.
When the goal is reached, you can withdraw the money and make your purchase or purchases. Or, in the case of an emergency fund, let it sit until you need it.

You now have a simple five-step strategy that works. It requires some discipline, as most long-term things do, but it's worth it.

Let's go through how to utilize this strategy for buying a home, buying a car, and funding higher education. These three items are major expenses and usually require a mix of cash and loans. We're not going to go into the nitty-gritty details and logistics of qualifying for loans to fund these three items. I'll cover each briefly and discuss the costs and fees you'll need to save up for each.

Buying a Home
In general, a move-in-ready home will cost hundreds of thousands of dollars and up. Most of us don't have a few hundred thousand lying around with which to purchase a home outright. It's not like walking into a store and picking something off a shelf. You're likely going to need to save for a down payment and get a mortgage, aka a home loan, for the remaining cost.

Outside of the down payment, there are other costs you will need cash on hand to handle when purchasing a home. You will need money for closing costs, which can range from 3% to 5% of the purchase price. Even move-in-ready homes will require some level of repairs or changes, so have that cash on hand. Money to furnish the house and likely do any interior design work you want, so it suits your tastes, is also needed. It's your home, your place of comfort and peace.

The advice is to put 20% down when purchasing a home. However, that isn't the only option. There are some programs and loan types where you can have a down payment of 0-3% of the purchase price. Save up and put as much as you can into the down payment while still accounting for the other costs. Aim for at least 3-5 percent.

However, with most lenders, the more money you have to put down, in other words, the closer you can get to the recommended 20% down, the better you look. Also, if you're able to put 20% down, you'll save money in two ways.

1) You won't have to pay PMI (private mortgage insurance). This can be up to 1.5% of the total loan amount per year. For example, let's say you took a $400,000 loan to purchase a home. The PMI would add $6,000 in costs per year.
2) You can take out a smaller loan that saves you on interest paid over the years.

Closing costs are typically 2-3%, and you'll need to have the cash in hand. Sometimes you can get the seller or the lender to pay the closing costs, but it's best to be prepared. Put the money for the down payment, closing costs, potential repairs, and furnishing in a separate savings account, not your checking account.

Assess how much home you can truly afford and if you're eligible for any home-buying programs in your area. Once this research is complete, you'll be able to estimate the range for the total amount needed for a down payment and closing costs. Work the savings strategy to achieve your goal amount.

Buying a Car
Cars can also cost five figures, and the average person doesn't have the cash on hand to buy one without a loan. If you do, kudos, pat yourself on the back, and celebrate that achievement. If you can save up and purchase a car, then I definitely advocate for that route. Can you say no car note! No increasing debt! Do that if you can. However, many people also don't have the time to save up all the funds needed to purchase a car, or aren't in a position to wait to save all the money. If this is you, then you may need to get financing in addition to saving.

Briefly, let's discuss car financing. You may get better financing terms from your bank or credit union than from the car dealer. The car dealer's interest rates are usually much higher. This is a mistake that many people make that ends up costing them a lot of money. Get a pre-approval quote for financing from a bank or credit union. You can use this quote at the dealership to negotiate, especially if you have great credit.

At the dealership, consider the total price of the car. The salesperson may only quote monthly payments because lower numbers sound better and more manageable. However, remember that those lower numbers are usually associated with a longer-term loan, so you'll be paying interest for much longer. In other words, you'll end up paying a much larger total price for the car. Therefore, it is better to consider what the total price will be. Remember your goal amount for the price of the car and don't go over it. Don't be swayed by a quote with a low monthly payment.

Once you've done your research and picked a car that fits your needs, you'll have an estimated range of how much you will need to save to purchase the car or make a reasonable down payment. Of course, the more money you can put down, the less you will need to finance and the more attractive you look to the lender.

Aim to save 10-20% of the vehicle's price as a down payment. There are some dealers who say you don't need any money down. You've likely seen or heard the commercials. However, let me reiterate. Saving a down payment is in your best interest. You'll have to finance less money, which means you'll also pay less in total because you're paying interest on a smaller amount of money. You'll also likely be able to negotiate a better interest rate. When you know how much you want to save, then implement the rest of the steps in the saving strategy.

Funding Higher Education

Higher education is another major expense many people eventually want to invest in for themselves or their children. However, it comes with a hefty price tag. For the 2024-2025 academic year, the College Board reports that the average cost of tuition and fees at a private college or university was **$43,350 per year**. For in-state residents at a public college or university, the average cost was **$11,610 per year**, and **$30,780 per year** for out-of-state residents. You'll need between $46,440 and $173,400 for the four years needed to complete a bachelor's degree. We haven't touched on graduate school or advanced higher education.

It can be difficult for most of us to save up this amount of money. I have read stories of some who have done it, but I think it's safe to say that's not the norm. While the average person likely can't save up the entire amount to pay all the tuition and fees for four years, it is very possible to save up for key items such as books, classroom supplies, room and board, meal plans, dorm supplies, travel around town, travel back and forth between campus and home, and other random incidentals. Save up as much as you can using the savings strategy. Couple that with the rest of your funding strategy.

Other funding and methods outside of student loans you can use in addition to your savings are:

1) Scholarships and grants.

You've definitely heard of this avenue. This is money you do not have to pay back. There are scholarships for all types of characteristics, like C students, left-handed students, students who have read a particular book, etc. Searching for scholarships is like searching for a job; you have to put in the hours and do the research. Apply and keep applying. Get help from someone who has mastered the system. There are several books and resources out there.

2) Start early with investment accounts.

If you're saving for a child's education, also use methods like a 529 plan, UPromise, or a regular (not education-specific) investment account. A 529 plan is an investment account for educational costs. With UPromise, you get cash back on everyday shopping that is deposited directly into a college savings plan, like a 529 plan, or you can simply request the money. These options let you leverage the power of compound interest to grow your money over the years, so you have a substantial sum to pay for educational costs. Set up an account as early as possible and contribute consistently.

3) Employment.

Many students pay for school by working and attending school part-time, or by taking a gap year(s) after high school before going to college. They work for a year or a couple of years to compile the money for tuition and pay for college that way. If you go the work first route, then make sure to plan to minimize expenses as much as possible so more of your check, hopefully almost all of it, can be set aside for tuition and fees. Common methods include living with parents or getting a few roommates, going without a car, etc.

4) Go to school in-state.

If you pick an in-state school (a school within the state where you live), you can decrease your college tuition by $12,000 or more per year. If it's an in-state public school, then you can save yourself from paying an additional $30,000 or more per year.

5) Employer Reimbursement Programs

Take advantage of programs at your job that will pay you to pursue higher education. Not only may they cover some of the costs, but this could also result in a raise later on as well.

6) Getting Financial Aid

You can also apply to receive financial aid from the college. If you're applying for yourself, then it's based solely on your income and assets. However, if you're applying for your child, you have to include information about your income and assets, as well as the student's income and assets. This information goes into the FAFSA (Free Application for Federal Student Aid). This information is used to calculate your expected family contribution (EFC) and how much the college will give in financial aid. The aid can be in the form of scholarships, grants, loans, or work study programs.

"The FAFSA" is not just one formula to determine EFC and how much aid the applicant is eligible to receive. There are two financial aid formulas.

1. FAFSA – free application for federal student aid
2. CSS Profile – college scholarship service profile

Each formula calculates your EFC differently. They weigh and consider various aspects of your assets. You can arrange your finances and assets to qualify for as much financial aid as possible.

The FAFSA
FAFSA is the easiest and most well-known assessment. This formula does not count the value of your home, farm, or small business. It also will not include any 529 savings plans controlled by someone other than the parent or the student. Income and assets are taxed at 5.6%. This means that if you have, let's say, $150,000 saved, your EFC increases by $8,400. However, the student's income and assets are taxed much higher at 20%!

Consider structuring your finances and assets to maximize your EFC. Here are some suggestions if the college uses the FAFSA. Remember to assess your individual situation.

1) Move your child's money to an account in your name and sell the assets.

You may think, "No, it's not mine," but with the money taxed at 20%, a lot of it would end up going to the school anyway, since they'll raise the EFC. Also, talk to a financial advisor and see if it's better to have them sell their assets and you move the money to a 529 plan.

2) Ask a relative you trust to control the 529 plan.

If grandma or grandpa controls the account, then it's excluded from the calculation. No matter how many thousands of dollars are in the plan, it's not included, and you can drastically lower your EFC.

The CSS PROFILE

Approximately 300 colleges use this. This calculation looks much more deeply into your assets. The formula includes your home equity, farms, business, annuities, and all 529 plans. Here are some suggestions for arranging your money and assets to maximize your EFC.

1) Hold off on purchasing a new property.

If it's time to fill out the information for financial aid, hold off on purchasing a new property if you can. Acquiring a new property can increase your EFC and lower your financial aid.

2) Don't have the student control the 529 plan.

If it's a student-controlled 529 plan, then the amount is taxed at 25%. However, if it is a parent-controlled plan, then it's only taxed at 5.6%. This will make a huge difference. You can drastically lower your EFC by making sure you're in control of the 529 plan.

3) Move the student's money to an account in your name.

Same as with the FAFSA, assets owned by the student are taxed at a much higher rate. The CSS Profile formula taxes them at 25%. Talk to a financial advisor and see if it's better to have them sell their assets and you move the money to a 529 plan.

Each formula also gives you a break if you have more than one child in college at the same time. They also do not include the money in your retirement accounts in the calculation of your EFC. Money already in retirement accounts is exempt, but any contributions you make while the student is in college are included in the calculation. If possible, contribute as much as you can to your retirement accounts before your child heads to college. Doing this will also be great for you because you will have more money compounding interest for longer.

By moving some money and assets around, you can significantly lower your EFC and maximize how much you receive in financial aid.

Chapter 11: Your Financial System

To acquire and best utilize money and assets, you will need a system that keeps things flowing in a way that allows you to progress toward financial goals. In this chapter, we're going to review what those things are and how they interconnect to make up your personal finance system.

Personal Money Strategy
Before you can successfully start making changes to accelerate your financial progress, you need to get organized. You need to strengthen the foundation for your finances. This schematic of your personal money strategy shows a good example of cash flow.

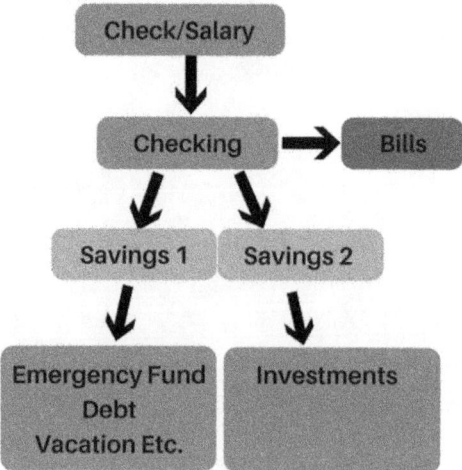

Check/Salary
↓
Checking → Bills
↓   ↓
Savings 1   Savings 2
↓   ↓
Emergency Fund   Investments
Debt
Vacation Etc.

Money comes in, likely from your paycheck or a side hustle. The money is distributed to pay expenses, grow savings, and increase investments. The cash flow schematic shows the four parts of your financial system.

Let's break down each part and the tools you need for each.

The parts of your financial system are:
1) Income - The money that comes into your household.

2) Household bills – Expenses to keep your household running smoothly, money flowing out.

3) Saving and growing your money - This part is money saved as well as money used to build wealth and acquire more assets.

4) Protect your assets - This part is about protecting everything you're building, your wealth.

Part 1 – Income: Maximize Your Paycheck
If employed and have a W-2 from another company, you have a paycheck. If self-employed, you have a paycheck or a consistent withdrawal. This is the money you can use to achieve your financial goals.

Therefore, it's crucial to use the tips presented in this book to maximize your income. For W-2 employees, to make sure you're getting the most money possible into your household, review the exemptions on your W-4 form. The W-4 is the form that you fill out when you start a job. It tells the company, your employer, how much federal tax to deduct from your pay. Some states use the federal form. Some states have a separate

136

state-specific form that is used to tell the state how much tax to withhold. The rest of the states don't have income tax.

The tax forms take into account the number of dependents you have and your marriage status. These forms are important to maximize your paycheck while minimizing your taxes. If you fill them out wrong, you'll end up owing taxes at the end of the year or allowing the government to take a lot of your money, which results in a big tax refund. You may be thinking, "ok, what's the problem with the tax refund?" Nothing really, but it would be better for you to have more of that money throughout the year that you can put towards your financial goals.

Don't claim too many exemptions, or you'll end up owing money during tax season. However, you also don't want to only put zero and have them take out the maximum in taxes, because then you have less money to use during the year.

As things change, such as when you have a child, get married, etc., fill out a new W-4 form to reflect the change in your situation. This may allow more money to come into your household to cover any new or increased expenses.

I'm also a big proponent of creating multiple streams of income. This is where a side hustle comes into play. If you lose your job or are furloughed, having a side hustle will help bring some money into your household. We know financial emergencies and unexpected expenses happen, as when the federal U.S. government shut down in October 2013, December 2018, and October 2025, when a budget for the new fiscal year wasn't approved. More than 800,000 people who worked for the federal government were furloughed. They couldn't work and did not get paid. Think about what would happen if your paycheck did not arrive ... and you didn't know when it would come.

Side hustle income would be extremely beneficial in helping you to continue to pay key household bills. Yes, you should still have an emergency fund, but supplementing that with side income is a great help. Also, if you can grow your side hustle income to at least cover essential household bills, you'd be in a great place. A side hustle isn't only about doom and gloom. It can also help you reach your financial goals faster.

As your paycheck and side hustle money come in, you'll need to know what to do with the money. One of the tools you need for this is one you're likely already using. A simple bank checking account. This will serve as the base for the rest of your cash flow as you move money around to achieve your financial goals.

Have your paycheck deposited directly into a bank checking account. This way, you are FDIC (Federal Deposit Insurance Corporation) insured for up to $250,000, which means that no matter what happens, the bank has to give you your money. Even if a natural disaster hits and takes out the bank, you can still get your money. If the money is stored in your house, it's gone.

Part 2 - Household Bills

The next part of your personal financial system is paying your expenses, especially your household bills.

It's important that you include a money calendar or another system to track when bills are due as part of your system. As you work on bettering your finances or work towards a large financial goal, make it a habit to know how much money will be leaving your checking account and when.

Use a money calendar. A money calendar is a calendar where you enter each bill and its due date. For example, on the 25th of the month, you may write the word rent and the dollar amount. It's likely your rent is due on the first, but write it as due and send it several days earlier so you can make sure to get it in on time. A money calendar gives you a great visual of when money will be going into and out of your checking account. It's essential not only to know how much money you have left, but also when the next bill is due, so you can keep your cash flow positive.

You don't need to know this information off the top of your head all the time. Who has room for that?! However, using a money calendar will give you something to check when you're considering making a purchase or are reviewing your finances.

Creating your money calendar isn't anything fancy or complicated. You can use your online calendar and add the bill as an event. You can then set the reminders for that bill event. Using an online calendar works well because it's always with you. You can check it at any time, which is especially useful when you're on the go.

Combine a digital calendar with a physical one. Having a dedicated money calendar helps simplify the view so those important financial dates don't get lost.

Part 3 – Where to Put Your Money

The next part of your personal financial system is where you store your money and the tools you use to grow your money. If you're not already, you should open a savings account to hold your emergency fund. Your emergency fund is a reserve of money to use in case of an actual emergency, such as a layoff, unexpected medical bills, a blown tire, or a cracked car windshield.

A complete emergency fund is 6-12 months' worth of bills set aside. For an entrepreneur, extend that to 18 months. Yes, that is quite a large sum of money. The majority of it still needs to be in a regular or high-yield savings account. Don't expect much growth. This is not your investment account. It's savings set aside in case of an emergency so you don't rack up debt when an emergency happens and you may need to get your hands on cash quickly.

To grow your money, you will be acquiring assets. These are the retirement and non-retirement investment accounts (and other assets) that you have. We'll be talking about putting money towards investments in step seven. There are a few things you should have in place before you're ready to invest.

Part 4 – Protect your assets
The last part of your personal finance system is protecting your assets. You're working hard to build wealth. You're working hard to put money away towards retirement, build your side hustle, achieve your financial goals, and create the lifestyle you desire.

You are a key element to your plans. You're the person working to earn the money. You're crucial to the cash flow. You need to make sure that you're protecting yourself and what you're building. We'll go into this deeper in step seven, about protecting your wealth. This includes protecting yourself and your cash flow.

To recap, make adjustments to your financial system to optimize it and reach your financial goals by:

1) maximizing income earned
2) staying aware of your household bills and how much money is going in and coming out

3) staying aware and utilizing accounts to store cash and grow your money

4) protecting your wealth

Step 5: The Leveraging Credit Blueprint

Chapter 12: The Credit Debt Cycle

Although the majority of us use credit every day, many are unclear about what their credit score is, how to maintain a good credit score, or how to raise it. In this chapter, we'll answer those questions about credit and credit scores.

It is so commonplace to use credit in America and many countries that we don't usually think about it anymore. We just assume that to afford higher-priced items, we have to use credit. You know things like what we discussed in step four: a car, a house, and higher education. It makes sense, since most of us don't have hundreds of thousands of dollars lying around to buy these items. Therefore, we use credit.

Credit is not inherently bad. It's about how you use credit and not letting it get out of control. Credit can be a powerful tool for building wealth. Let's discuss what a lender assesses before granting a loan.

Briefly, the things a lender looks for are:

1) Capacity
They need to determine if you have the financial resources to pay a mortgage. Usually, lenders want to see at least two years of steady work history with a reliable paycheck. If you're self-employed or have a job that works on commission, then you're likely going to have to provide more documentation to show you can repay a loan.

2) Credit history

They want to see that you make timely payments on the current debt you already have. They don't want your debt-to-income ratio to be too high. It needs to be less than 43%. Otherwise, they may not feel comfortable that you can handle a new loan. They also look to determine if you've had credit for a while and handled it well. They look at your credit age. That's why you're cautioned not to open new lines of credit right before trying to get a loan.

3) Collateral

Collateral is an asset you own that can be used to secure the loan. It is used if you don't pay the loan, and they need to seize your property to recover the costs. For example, you can use the home as collateral to obtain a mortgage.

4) Capital

This also shows that you can afford to repay the loan. Having cash reserves shows this. It doesn't look good if you get a large cash gift from a relative, because it's a one-time infusion of cash. It's not a deal-breaker but it isn't optimal.

Basically, they want to make sure you can and will repay the loan. Therefore, it is important to start months in advance, making regular deposits into the account that you will share as proof with the underwriter. The underwriter is the bank employee who assesses whether you'll be approved for a loan.

Buying a home is one of the tools to build wealth. We have already talked about when a house becomes a true asset. If you need a car to get to work, to make money so you can survive, and you don't have thousands of dollars in the bank, then credit, or in other words, financing, comes to the rescue, and that's ok. Or let's say you're starting up a side hustle that you will turn into a small business. While I encourage bootstrapping it, many people also use credit to help get it off the ground. For example, some new entrepreneurs use credit to purchase key equipment or materials.

Credit can be a powerful tool for building wealth when used responsibly. This is when credit is used to purchase a need for survival (like a car) and when it is used to acquire an asset. Remember, an asset is something that increases in value over time.

Another reason to be very responsible with credit is that others also use that credit data to make decisions concerning you. If you want to get credit, lenders check your credit history. A landlord will run a credit check to determine whether they'll rent to you. Some employers will do a credit check prior to hiring you.

Who Creates Your Credit Report?
The lenders report data about your credit use and habits to the three major credit bureaus: TransUnion, Equifax, and Experian. This data is shown on your credit report.

These three bureaus use this data to calculate your credit score. The main algorithm used to determine your credit score is the FICO formula; however, there are derivatives. Your credit score is basically the number other lenders use to decide whether they should extend credit or, in other words, loan money to you.

Credit Score Factors
Your credit score is based on several different factors. They're not weighted equally, meaning some factors have a larger impact on your credit score than others.

Factor 1: Payment History, 35%
They look at your history of paying your bills. Do you pay bills on time? They assess your credit and whether you have made timely payments on those debt accounts.

Factor 2: Amount Owed, 30%
They look at the amount you owe relative to your available credit. If you have used up a lot of your available credit, this may indicate that you're likely to miss or make late payments. This is called credit utilization.

Factor 3: Type of Credit, 10%
The types of credit you have are also accounted for in your credit score. They analyze the mix of credit types, e.g., credit cards, retail credit cards, student loans, and mortgage loans. The mix isn't as important as making sure you pay each in a timely manner.

Factor 4: New Credit, 10%

The amount of new credit you have is also assessed. Don't open many new credit lines or accounts in a short amount of time, or else you'll seem overextended and indicate that you'll be likely to make late payments or miss payments.

Factor 5: Length of Credit History, 15%

The length of your credit history is also factored into your credit score. A longer history will improve your credit score if it shows responsible credit use. Responsible use of credit can be assessed using the four factors mentioned previously, including timely payments.

As you can see, paying your bills on time and maintaining a low debt-to-credit ratio have the greatest impact on your credit score. Pay on time and keep your utilization low.

Credit Score

Credit scores range from 300 to 850. The higher your score, the better your credit and the better your credit management skills are viewed. Each lender has their own system of determining your risk level based on your credit score. The lender determines what credit score range it considers good, acceptable, or high risk. However, in general, a credit score of 720 and above is a good credit score, while a score below 580 is considered high risk. An excellent credit score means you're above 800. This is in general. Whether you're approved or not really depends on the lender. Let's dive deeper.

How to Interpret Your Credit Score
As explained, your credit score is one of the most powerful numbers in your financial life. Understanding what your score means gives you the power to negotiate better rates, qualify for more opportunities, and strengthen your overall financial health.

What the Numbers Really Mean
Poor Credit (300–579)
A score in this range tells lenders that you may have had significant credit challenges, such as late payments, collections, high credit utilization, or limited credit history.

What it means:
- You may be denied for loans or credit cards.
- If approved, you'll likely receive the highest interest rates and lowest credit limits.
- Even non-lenders, like landlords, cellphone companies, and utility providers, may require higher deposits.

This isn't a permanent label. With consistent positive habits, you can climb out of this range faster than you think.

Fair Credit (580–669)

This range signals mixed financial behaviors. You may be rebuilding credit or establishing it.

What it means:
- You can qualify for more products, but interest rates will still be higher than ideal.
- You may face limits on the amount you can borrow.
- Lenders see you as a "moderate risk" borrower.

This is the "in-progress" zone. With a few key adjustments, such as on-time payments or reducing credit utilization, your score can quickly rise into the next tier.

Good Credit (670–739)
You'll likely be considered to have solid, responsible credit   behavior.

What it means:
- You qualify for most loans, credit cards, and financing options.
- Interest rates and terms are generally favorable.
- Lenders see you as a reliable borrower.

Once you reach this range, the goal is to maintain this strong foundation with consistent habits.

Very Good Credit (740–799)

You're seen as a low-risk borrower, and lenders trust that you manage financial obligations responsibly.

What it means:
- You receive better-than-average interest rates.
- You gain access to premium credit products, higher limits, and more flexibility.
- You're positioned to build wealth through lower borrowing costs.

Excellent Credit (800–850)
This is elite territory. Scores in this range demonstrate exceptional money management.

What it means:
- You're likely to receive the best interest rates, the highest credit limits, and the strongest negotiating power.
- You save thousands over time on mortgages, car loans, and personal loans.
- Lenders see you as extremely low risk.

This category doesn't require perfection. It simply reflects long-term consistency with paying on time, keeping balances low, and avoiding unnecessary new credit.

What Your Credit Score Tells Lenders About You
In one glance, a lender learns:
- How consistently you pay bills
- How much of your available credit you use

152

- How long you've used credit
- How often you apply for new credit
- How well you've managed different types of accounts

Your score helps them predict: *"If we lend you money, what's the likelihood you'll pay us back on time, every time?"*

Increasing Your Credit Score

If your score has already dipped out of the good range, then you'll want to work on bringing it back up.

1) Pay your bills on time.

We talked about how this has the biggest influence on your score. Making timely payments is one of the most important ways to increase your score. A recent late payment can drop your credit score by several points. A missed payment is much worse. Missing or skipping a payment on a debt account can drop your credit score by 50 points or more. If you sometimes think "I'll skip this payment and just try to double up next month," ... DON'T. Pay at least the minimum amount and then double the payment next month. It's much better to make the payment and keep your credit score intact.

2) Get your credit utilization to less than 30%.

We discussed that the amount you owe relative to your available credit is the second-largest factor in calculating your credit score. If you've maxed out your credit cards, it decreases your credit score. If you haven't quite maxed out credit cards, but you've used up a lot of your available credit, then your score decreases as well.

For example, if you have a $15,000 limit on a credit card and have charged $12,000 on that card, you've used 80% of your available credit. This will decrease your credit score and signal to lenders that you are most likely overextended and may make late payments or miss payments altogether. If this is you, work on paying down your credit cards so that your credit utilization (credit limit to amount owed ratio) is less than 30%. Your credit score will gradually increase.

3) Don't open any new lines of credit.

The number of new lines of credit is also considered when calculating your credit score. If you need to raise your credit score, do not open new lines of credit. For example, when you're in the store checking out, and the cashier asks you if you would like to open a store card to save 10%, tell her no. Those store cards are credit cards and will be reflected in your credit history. Maintain the lines of credit you already have and work to pay down their balances. You'll decrease your debt and raise your credit score. A win-win situation.

4) Correct any errors.

Your credit report may contain errors that are negatively impacting your credit score. Review your credit report and ensure that everything in the report is accurate and reflects loans you recognize.

Understanding Your Credit Report
Your credit report shows your credit history, which is all the lines of credit you have had over the past ten years. There are several sections in the report.

1) Personal Identifying Information
This section includes:
- Full legal name and any variations (married names, misspellings, or aliases)
- Birth date
- Current and previous home addresses
- Social Security number variations
- Employer history (optional and based on what lenders provide)

Although this information does not affect your credit score, it is essential for accurately matching the report to you.

Why This Section Matters
- Incorrect personal information can signal identity theft.
- Mixed files, when someone else's credit data appears on your report, it often shows errors in this section.

- Outdated addresses can be clues to unauthorized accounts opened elsewhere.

2) Credit Accounts (Tradelines)
Credit accounts, also called tradelines are the backbone of a credit report. Each account you've opened in the last seven to ten years is listed here. It shows:
- Account type (credit card, mortgage, auto loan, student loan, personal loan, etc.)
- Creditor or lender name
- Account number (partially masked for security)
- Date the account was opened
- Credit limit or original loan amount
- Current balance
- Payment history, month by month
- Account status (open, closed, paid, charged-off, past due)
- Responsibility type (individual, joint, authorized user, etc.)

Why This Section Matters
Your payment history and credit utilization come directly from this section. Late payments, charge-offs, and defaulted loans appear here and can significantly impact your score.

3) Public Records
Only a narrow set of public records appear in modern credit reports, primarily:
- Bankruptcies
  - Chapter 7 (reported for 10 years)

o   Chapter 13 (reported for 7 years)

Civil judgments and liens were removed from credit reports in 2017 as part of the National Consumer Assistance Plan, so they should no longer appear on credit reports.

Why This Section Matters
Bankruptcies can be major negative items that affect your ability to obtain credit and the cost of borrowing. Ensuring the information is accurate and timely is critical.

4) Collection Accounts
Any account that a creditor sends to a third-party collection agency appears in this section. These listings typically show:
- Name of the collection agency
- Name of original creditor
- Original balance and current balance
- Date the debt went into collections
- Account status (unpaid, paid, settled)

Collections can remain on your credit report for seven years from the date of first delinquency, *not* from when the debt was sold or updated. Understanding this timeline is essential to knowing when an item should fall off.

5) Credit Inquiries
There are two types of inquiries, hard and soft.

Hard inquiries
- Occur when you apply for a credit card, personal loan, car financing, mortgage, or some apartment leases
- Are visible to lenders
- Can slightly lower your score
- Stay on your report for 24 months (impact typically lasts 12 months)

Soft inquiries
- Occur during pre-approvals, insurance checks, employment checks, or when checking your own credit
- Not visible to lenders
- Do not affect your score

Why This Section Matters
A large number of hard inquiries within a short period can suggest risk to lenders. Unrecognized inquiries can also be a sign of attempted identity theft.

Different types of information are removed at slightly different times.

1) Credit accounts
Your credit accounts, which are credit cards and other loans, stay on your report for up to ten years after the last date of activity. Therefore, even after you pay off a loan, it will remain on your credit report for ten years after that last payment.

If you didn't pay off the loan, then that negative "mark" remains on your credit report for seven years after it became past due. Late payments show up on your credit report for seven years, too.

2) Bankruptcy

A Chapter 7, Chapter 11, and dismissed Chapter 13 bankruptcy stays on your credit report for ten years. A discharged chapter 13 bankruptcy, which means the bankruptcy went through and your dischargeable debts are released, remains on your credit report for seven years.

Chapter 13: How to Review Your Credit Report

Reviewing Your Credit Report

Therefore, when viewing your credit report, you can see all your lines of credit as well as any negative information that may still be on your report. Things that lower your credit score are called negative marks or negative information.

As a reminder, you can go to credit monitoring sites to get access to your credit report. It's free to sign up and see your information. They'll even show you your credit score from at least two of the three major credit bureaus. You can also get your credit report from the three major credit bureaus: Equifax, TransUnion, and Experian once a year for free. You can also now go to annualcreditreport.com to receive free weekly reports from all three bureaus.

Your credit score will be slightly different between the credit bureaus. This is due to reporting and somewhat different algorithms. Each bureau compiles your financial data from lenders, collection agencies, and public records, such as bankruptcy filings. These are publicly available court records.

Not every lender has to report to all three credit bureaus. So if it reports to only two, you can see how that may create three different scores.

You should review your credit report from the official three major credit bureaus at a minimum every twelve months. You could even space it out and order one from one bureau every four months. This way, you can look at an official report from a major credit bureau every four months.

You can conduct constant reviews using other online sites, as well as your credit card statement if your credit card company offers it. Some credit card companies have taken to posting your score on your statement.

You want to keep reviewing your credit report and credit score to make sure there are no errors and you're making progress with your credit management. An error would be anything showing up on your credit report that is not true, that is not supposed to be there. It's essential to get these removed, as they can affect your credit score.

Analyzing Your Credit Reports
Here's what you need to review as you analyze your credit report.

Step 1: Verify Personal Information
Check for:
- Misspelled names
- Incorrect addresses
- Addresses you don't recognize
- Employment information you don't recognize
- SSN variations that don't match yours

Why it's important:
Identity errors often result in mixed files, where someone else's account ends up on your report. This can also indicate identity theft.

Step 2: Review Each Credit Account Carefully
For every credit account:
- Do you recognize the account?
- Is the account type correct?
- Is the open date accurate?
- Is the credit limit correct?
- Is the balance accurate?
- Are payment statuses correct (especially late payments)?
- Is the account marked "closed" if it was closed?
- Has the creditor reported the account multiple times?

Red Flags to Look For
- Incorrect late payments
- Credit limits reported lower than they actually are (raises utilization)
- Accounts you paid off still showing balances
- "Re-aged" accounts (the date of first delinquency has been changed illegally)
- Accounts marked incorrectly, such as saying "charged-off" when they were settled
- Accounts showing as "open" even though they were closed

Step 3: Examine Your Payment History

Payment history is the largest factor in your credit score. Look through the month-by-month grid:

- Are there any 30, 60, or 90-day late marks that are incorrect?
- Were there billing issues that could explain a late mark?
- Do any late payments appear after a settled dispute with the lender?

If you always pay on time, even one incorrect delinquency mark can significantly lower your score.

Step 4: Review Collection Accounts Thoroughly
Check for:

- Collections you don't recognize
- Balances that seem inflated
- Paid collections still showing balances
- Duplicate collection entries (original creditor and collector both listing the same debt)
- Incorrect dates
- Accounts that should have aged off

If a debt collector "refreshes" or "re-ages" an account to keep it on your report longer, this is a violation.

Step 5: Review Public Records
Only bankruptcies should appear. If you see any other public records, tax liens, civil judgments, or lawsuits, they should be disputed immediately.

Step 6: Examine Credit Inquiries

Look for:

- Unauthorized hard inquiries
- Any signs of fraud, e.g., attempted credit applications
- Excessive inquiries from a single day

If you did not authorize a credit application, dispute the inquiry and consider freezing your credit.

Top Things to Check Every Time You Review Your Credit Report

1. Accuracy of your personal information
2. Accounts you don't recognize
3. Incorrect late payments
4. Incorrect balances or credit limits
5. Duplicate accounts or duplicate collections
6. Accounts reporting past the 7-year limit
7. Hard inquiries you didn't authorize
8. Accounts incorrectly showing as open or active
9. Fraudulent accounts opened in your name
10. Inconsistent information between bureaus

This checklist alone can help you detect most issues before they cause harm.

How to Spot Errors on a Credit Report

Credit report errors are more common than many people realize. Errors usually fall into three categories:

1) Identity Errors

These occur when the report includes information about another person, or your identity information is wrong. Examples:

- Incorrect or unfamiliar name
- Incorrect SSN variations
- Wrong addresses
- Accounts that belong to someone with a similar name
- Fraudulent accounts

2) Account Errors

These are the most common and can significantly hurt your score.
Examples:

- Payments reported late that were on time
- Incorrect balances
- Wrong credit limits
- Accounts you closed but are listed as open
- Accounts listed as delinquent that are not
- Duplicate reporting
- Re-aged accounts

3) Reporting Errors

These are errors where the reporting itself is outdated or incorrect.
Examples:

- Accounts older than 7 years still appear
- Bankruptcies reporting longer than allowed
- Collections that were paid but still show balances
- Incorrect dates of last activity

What to Do If You Find an Error on Your Credit Report

You have the right to dispute and correct inaccurate information. The dispute process is your legal protection against unfair reporting. Here's the process:

Step 1: Gather Evidence

You'll need documentation that proves the item is incorrect, such as:

- Payment receipts or bank statements
- Letters from creditors
- Settlement agreements
- Police reports (for identity theft)
- ID documents
- Any written communication relevant to the account

Make copies of everything; never send your only original document.

Step 2: File a Dispute with Each Credit Bureau

You must dispute with the bureau showing the error. If all three show the error, you must submit to all three.

Although bureaus allow online, phone, and mail disputes, mail is the strongest method because it creates a paper trail.

Send your dispute by certified mail with a return receipt to:

- Equifax
- Experian
- TransUnion

Your dispute letter should include:

- Your full name, address, and report number (if available)
- A clear statement of what you are disputing
- Why the information is incorrect
- The correction or action you are requesting
- Copies (not originals) of supporting documents

Step 3: File a Direct Dispute with the Furnisher

The furnisher is the organization that reported the information (creditor, lender, collection agency, etc.). Send them:

- A copy of your bureau dispute
- All supporting documents
- A request that they investigate the accuracy of the report

This step is important because the bureau will contact the furnisher, who must verify the data.

Step 4: Wait for the Investigation

The credit bureau has:

- 30 days to investigate
- Up to 45 days if you send additional information during the investigation

They must:

- Investigate your dispute
- Contact the furnisher
- Correct, update, or delete the information

168

- Send you written results
- Provide a free updated credit report if changes were made

Step 5: Verify the Results

Once the investigation is complete, review your updated report. If the issue was corrected, great.

If the error was *not* corrected:

- File a second dispute with additional documentation
- File a complaint with the Consumer Financial Protection Bureau (CFPB)
- Consider adding a consumer statement to your report
- If it's identity theft, file a police report and place a fraud alert

Final Thoughts: Why Reviewing Your Credit Report Matters

Mistakes on your credit report can cost you thousands of dollars over your lifetime:

- Higher interest rates
- Denied loans
- Higher insurance premiums
- Lost housing opportunities
- Delayed employment offers

By reviewing your credit reports regularly, understanding what to look for, and knowing how to dispute errors, you protect your financial future.

Chapter 14: Debt elimination

Figuring out how to pay off debt can be daunting. Never mind actually paying it off. You may be following the advice of paying more than the minimum. You're doing that across all your debt accounts, but you're not seeing the progress you want. If you're stuck at the stage of "how in the world am I going to pay this off," then you'll get a lot out of this chapter. In this chapter, we'll discuss a simple method to create your debt reduction strategy.

Common Debt

In the previous chapter, you learned how to obtain and analyze your credit report. Therefore, you're familiar with your debt. You're ready to create a debt reduction strategy to eliminate your debt.

The average American has four different types of debt: student loans, auto loans, mortgage loans, and credit cards. Some people also have personal loans and medical debt. This can add up to a lot of debt. You calculated your debt-to-income ratio, so you know how much of your income goes toward debt. You also saw your WISE Score and know your overall financial fitness in the credit and debt category.

Let's improve these numbers using the elimination methods below.

Snowball Method

Here is the snowball method. You'll quickly see why it has the name that it does.

1) Stop using credit.

To eliminate debt, you have to stop accruing more. Don't take out any more loans. Don't use credit cards. Don't finance anything; that's a loan. Don't use store cards, as those are like credit cards.

2) Create a debt priority list.

Put your debt accounts in order from smallest to largest. This is the order in which you will pay off your debt. You will aggressively target your debt accounts by working your way through this list. Large debts, such as a mortgage or student loan, will have a lower interest rate than smaller debts, such as a credit card.

This is good and what you want, because debt with higher interest rates accrues faster. The average credit card interest rate has increased to over 20%. The average interest rates for other types of loans usually range between 5% and 28%. The rate you can lock in is dependent on your credit score. The better your credit score, the lower the interest rate you can get for your loan.

3) Pay more than the minimum on one debt account at a time.

Use the debt priority list you created in the previous step. This shows which debt you will pay more than the minimum on first. Pay the minimum on all the other debts on the list. Don't ignore any of your debt accounts, or you'll get those negative marks we just discussed on your credit report and cause your credit score to plummet. Target the debt account with the lowest minimum first, pay more than the minimum on that debt account, while paying the minimum payment on all other debt accounts.

4) Add the payment to the next step.
Once you've paid off that first debt, take the money that you were putting towards that debt and add it to the minimum payment of the next debt account on your list. Continue paying the minimum payment on all other debts.

5) Repeat until you eliminate all your debt.

The snowball method for debt elimination is not the only method available. There are a couple of others to consider.

Avalanche Method
The avalanche method differs from the snowball method because it targets the debts with the highest interest rates first. When you create your priority list, order the debt accounts by interest rate instead of the amount. The biggest interest rate goes first, while the smallest interest rate is last.

This method helps you save more money by tackling the debt that is growing fastest first. This method has the potential to save more money than the snowball method. However, if the debt with the highest interest rate is large, it can take a while to pay off, which can negatively affect your motivation.

The snowball method creates faster wins and the feeling that you're making significant progress. Therefore, it provides a boost of motivation that may take longer to achieve with the avalanche method.

Debt snowflake

This method involves taking unexpected extra money and putting that towards paying down debt. For example, say you unexpectedly saved $15 by not having to buy lunch, or you accumulated $20 in cash back savings. You would put that amount towards debt. While this strategy doesn't have as large an impact as the previous two methods, each unexpected extra payment can add up just as snowflakes pile up to create a blanket of snow.

The debt snowflake method can be used on its own. This is great for when money is tight or you need more flexibility. It can also be used together with the debt snowball or avalanche method to make a larger impact, faster.

Keys to Success

The methods outlined above are simple. It's the implementation of the methods that can be problematic. It takes work to stick to the process. It takes discipline to keep paying down your debt month after month for a few years. It's not going to be quick. However, here are a few key tips for success.

1) Have an emergency fund set up.

We talked about creating your financial goals and went through some good goals to aim for, with an emergency fund at the top. If you don't have money set aside for the inevitable emergency, you will end up reaching for a credit card or taking out a loan. A credit card is not an emergency fund. If that is your current fallback plan, then start saving whatever you can in a savings account.

2) Use motivational tricks.

We went over some motivational tricks that will help you stick to your budget. These tricks can also help you stick to your debt-reduction strategy. While it can take a while to pay off debt, it's possible and worth it. When you're not feeling great about your debt elimination journey, have a ready list of ways to re-motivate or energize yourself to keep going.

3) Project your debt-free date.

Use your strategy and debt repayment calculators to estimate when you will be done paying off your debt. There are plenty of debt repayment calculators. Keep your debt-free date on a vision board or other visible place. When you get frustrated, you can see it and be motivated by when you will be able to say you're debt-free.

4) Celebrate and pat yourself on the back when you knock out each debt.

For each debt elimination method, you'll have intermediary milestones on your path to debt freedom. Celebrating milestones along the way will help keep you motivated to achieve the ultimate goal of debt freedom. For example, let's say you paid off 75% of a debt, celebrate your progress. It's not done, but you will have made significant progress. You're working hard, so take a moment to recognize and celebrate your win.

5) Analyze your lifestyle and determine ways to free up money from your current budget.

Review your budget and ask yourself … What can be decreased? What can be eliminated? You already went through your budget and revised it. Take a second look at your budget and determine whether there is any more money to be found. When it's time to start the debt-reduction strategy, put this "found" money toward the debt.

Let's go over an example so you can see it in action. Let's say you have the following debts:
1) $15,000 in student loans
2) $5,000 on a credit card
3) $4,000 car loan
4) $100 on a retail store card
5) $300 medical bill

1) The first step is not to rack up any more debt. Therefore, you're not going to finance or charge absolutely anything else.

2) We'll use the debt snowball method. We're going to create a priority list by ordering them from smallest to largest.
   1) $100 on a retail store card
   2) $300 medical bill
   3) $4,000 car loan ($150 payment)
   4) $5,000 on a credit card ($200 payment)
   5) $15,000 in student loans ($115 payment)

After streamlining your budget, you found another $200 to put toward debt. That means in one month you can knock out the $100 on the retail card and put $100 extra on the medical bill. One debt is gone! In the second month, you can take the full $200 and knock out the remaining $200 on the medical bill. The second debt is gone.

You start a side hustle and now have an additional $500 per month to put towards the debt. Now you have $700 to add to the $150 you were paying on your car loan. Therefore, you pay $850 per month toward your car loan, and in less than a year, that can be eliminated. The third debt is gone.

Now roll that $850 amount to the next debt. You would add $850 + $200, for a total of $1,050 per month, to your credit card payment.

See how this works. You'll save a lot of money that you otherwise would have paid in interest. If you stay focused and keep putting more and more money toward your debt, you'll eliminate it much faster.

Step 6: The Financial Independence Formula

Chapter 15: Preparing to Invest

Accumulating assets is crucial to your wealth strategy. You cannot save your way to wealth. You need to own things that appreciate and increase in value. In the previous chapters, I explained in detail how creating a money strategy will help you consistently save money and eliminate debt. We discussed why this is important to your financial stability and financial security. If you only do those things, you will be financially stable if you have income. As long as you are working and getting a paycheck and following those financial rules, you can maintain your financial stability.

However, you want to move past financial stability to financial freedom. You want to thrive, not just survive. Savings alone will not allow you to build wealth and leave a substantial legacy, because cash loses its buying power over time. This is why there is a cutoff to your emergency fund, which is cash sitting in a bank account. Inflation eats away at the spending power of that cash. You have to build wealth to have enough money to
- support your desired lifestyle,
- create time-freedom,
- have money to last for over 30 years of retirement,
- and leave a legacy such as generational wealth.

Unless you win $1 billion through a lottery, you can't save enough cash to build financial wealth. You have to acquire assets and take advantage of compound interest as the value increases over time. Compound interest is when you reinvest the money earned from interest back into the principal investment, allowing the new total to continue to accrue interest. Remember, we went over the snowball method of debt elimination, which works so well because the amount applied to the debt increases, paying it off faster. Compound interest is similar in that the amount that accrues interest grows because the amount made gets added back to the original amount you invested.

Let's compare two people. Person A *saves* one hundred dollars per month for 20 years, and Person B *invests* one hundred dollars per month for 20 years. At the end of the 20 years, Person A saved a total of $24,220.90 in a traditional bank savings account at 0.05%. However, Person B accumulated a total of $61,952.58, assuming an average 9% annual return. Although Person A and Person B each put the same dollar amount aside per month, the individual who invested for 20 years and got a 9% return on their investment has more than double the amount of money.

This is the power of investing, or in other words, purchasing assets. The money you put into investments compounds, making you a lot more money.

To prepare for retirement, you'll use your employer-sponsored investment accounts and individual investment accounts. Determine how much you need in retirement and then design a strategy to achieve that number. This dollar amount should be the bare minimum for your investment plan. Also consider how you can surpass that number so that you have wealth to pass on to the next generation. If you want to create generational wealth, then you need an overflow of assets that will not be completely used up during your retirement.

In the previous example comparing Person A and Person B, you can see that the amount of money invested is not enough to be comfortable in retirement. The person who only saved money would be able to live for one year with monthly expenses of $2,000. The person who invested would be able to live for two years and a few months. If you want to be able to survive the entirety of a 20 to 30-year retirement, then you have to determine how much money you need to invest per month per year until your retirement. You don't want to retire having worked for decades and not be able to survive.

According to the National Council on Aging, 45% of the elderly cannot afford basic expenses, and 80% wouldn't survive a financial disruption such as the death of a spouse, an illness, or the need for long-term care. You can avoid this with proper financial planning and strategy ... and time for the strategy to work.

To determine the amount of money you need to live comfortably in retirement, you will need to consider
- your current age,
- the age at which you plan to retire,
- how much you currently make,

- how much you put towards retirement every month, and
- how much you expect to spend per month in retirement.

When you invest, there is always a risk. In other words, there is a chance that you can lose some of the money you invested or all of it. This is why you should ensure you have a solid financial foundation before aggressively investing. You must be financially stable. This means that you've met certain criteria.

You should have at least three months of bills saved in an emergency fund. We've talked about the importance of an emergency fund before, so I won't go into it again. You also need to get rid of any consumer debt. Most consumer debt has high interest rates. Therefore, they will grow faster than your wealth-building vehicles. A reasonable return on investment for investing over time is about 8%. Therefore, any consumer debt that is above 7% should be paid off before you consider investing heavily. This applies to non-retirement investing.

Your Investing Goal
Your reason for investing will partly determine your investment strategy. Get clear on why you're investing, how soon you will need the money, and your level of risk tolerance.

Before you begin investing, it's essential to have a clear roadmap, a plan that connects your money to your goals. Investing without direction is like driving without a destination. You may make progress, but you won't know if you're moving toward your goal. And what truly matters to you. Start by asking yourself a few key questions: 0

- Why am I investing?
- How soon will I need the money?
- How comfortable am I with taking risks?

Your answers will shape the type of investments that best fit your needs.

If your goal is to build or supplement an **emergency fund**, you'll want to prioritize safety and liquidity. These funds should be easily accessible in case of an unexpected event, so short-term options like high-yield savings accounts or money market funds are ideal.

If you're saving to **buy a home** within the next three to ten years, your investment strategy should balance growth with protection against market downturns. Exchange-Traded Funds (ETFs) and balanced portfolios, which combine stocks and bonds, can help your money grow while still managing risk.

For **retirement**, you typically have ten to forty years lead time which gives your investments room to compound and recover from short-term market fluctuations. This is great for stocks, index funds, and REITs (Real Estate Investment Trusts), which offer higher potential returns over time.

If you're investing for **college savings**, you also likely have a long lead time. A 529 plan is one of the best vehicles available. It offers tax advantages and can hold a mix of investments such as index funds, allowing your contributions to grow tax-free when used for qualified education expenses.

Finally, if your goal is **financial independence or early retirement (FIRE)**, your focus will be on building income-generating and growth-oriented assets. Index funds, real estate, and other cash-flow-producing investments can help you reach the point where your money works harder than you do.

By clarifying your goals and aligning your investment choices with your timeline and risk tolerance, you'll create a personalized roadmap that guides every financial decision and keeps you motivated throughout the journey.

Ready to Invest Checklist
Once you have achieved the items below, you are ready to invest and grow your assets aggressively.
- Intermediate emergency fund
- Low to no debt
- 401(k) or similar employer-based retirement investing account
- Sufficient discretionary income

Chapter 16: Starting to Invest

I feel confident that I've drilled home the point that saving is vital to financial success. However, when it comes to building wealth, saving alone is not enough. Inflation quietly erodes your savings over time. While the total dollars remain the same, the purchasing power decreases. The true path to building wealth is through **investing**. Whether you have $50 or $50,000, investing allows your money to grow through the power of compound interest, earning returns on your returns.

Let's walk you through everything you need to know to get started, from understanding different investment vehicles to setting up accounts, tracking progress, and even crafting a personalized strategy for financial independence and retirement.

Investing means using your money to buy assets that can grow in value or generate income. Over time, those assets can significantly outpace inflation and build real wealth. There are two ways investments make money. One is capital appreciation: the value of your investment increases, e.g., the stock price increases. The other is income generation, e.g., receiving dividends, interest, or rental income.

Here are some of the different investment vehicles, or in other words, ways to acquire assets. Those assets can include:

- **Stocks:** Ownership shares in a company.
- **Bonds:** Loans you make to governments or corporations in exchange for interest.

- **ETFs (Exchange-Traded Funds):** Bundles of assets (like stocks or bonds) that trade like a stock.
- **Mutual Funds:** Professionally managed portfolios of assets that investors buy into collectively. **REITs (Real Estate Investment Trusts):** Companies that own or finance income-producing real estate.
- **Commodities:** Physical goods like gold, oil, or agricultural products.
- **Alternative Assets:** Cryptocurrencies, collectibles, private equity, etc.

The key goal is to build a *diversified portfolio*, which is a mix of investment types that reduce risk while maximizing growth potential. You should design an investment strategy, with the help of a financial advisor if possible. This means you have a strategy or the assets that you will acquire and your asset allocation. Asset allocation is the different types of assets and what percentage of each type of asset will make up your investment portfolio. When designing this strategy, you have to take into account your time until retirement, your risk tolerance, and your long-term goals. Talking to a financial advisor is a great idea when creating your investment strategy.

Let's go into more detail about each type of investment.

Understanding the different types of investments is essential to building a balanced and resilient portfolio.

Each asset class plays a unique role in helping you grow wealth, manage risk, and achieve your financial goals. Knowing what each one does and how it fits into your overall plan allows you to invest with confidence and clarity.

Stocks represent ownership in a company, giving you a stake in its profits and growth. When you buy a stock, you're essentially purchasing a small piece of that business. Stocks carry a higher risk, as their prices can fluctuate significantly, but they also offer some of the highest potential returns over time, historically averaging 7–10% per year. Stocks are ideal for long-term investors who can ride out short-term market ups and downs in exchange for strong growth potential.

Bonds, on the other hand, are loans you make to a company or government in exchange for regular interest payments. They're generally lower-risk investments that provide steady, predictable income. However, they deliver lower returns than stocks. Bonds can serve as a stabilizing force in your portfolio, helping to offset the volatility of stocks. They're particularly valuable for diversification and for investors who prioritize stability or are approaching retirement.

Exchange-Traded Funds (ETFs) offer an easy way to invest in a bundle of assets, such as an index of the top 500 U.S. companies (the S&P 500), without buying each one individually. ETFs provide instant diversification, low fees, and the flexibility to trade throughout the day like stocks. They're an excellent choice for new investors because they simplify the investing process while providing broad market exposure.

Mutual Funds are professionally managed collections of stocks, bonds, or other assets. These funds are often used in employer-sponsored retirement plans and IRAs. While they can have higher management fees compared to ETFs, they're convenient for investors who prefer to delegate investment decisions to professionals. Mutual funds are well-suited for long-term investors who value diversification and expert management.

If you're interested in real estate but don't want the responsibilities of direct ownership, **Real Estate Investment Trusts (REITs)** provide a powerful alternative. REITs pool investor money to buy, manage, and finance income-producing properties such as apartment complexes, office buildings, or shopping centers. They generate dividends from rental income, making them a great way to add real estate exposure and consistent cash flow to your portfolio without becoming a landlord.

For those who want to own physical property, **direct real estate investing** can offer long-term appreciation, rental income, and valuable tax deductions. This might include buying and managing rental properties, flipping houses, or investing in vacation homes. While real estate can provide steady income and tangible assets, it typically requires more capital upfront and active management to succeed.

Finally, **alternative investments**, such as cryptocurrencies, commodities, collectibles, and private equity, are high-risk options best suited for experienced investors who already have a strong core portfolio. These assets can offer significant upside potential but also come with higher volatility and uncertainty. They should only make up a small portion of your overall investment mix.

By understanding how each of these investment types works, you can build a portfolio that balances growth, stability, and flexibility, helping you move steadily toward your financial goals.

Also, you need to have money to invest. The previous chapters have prepared you to free up more of your income to save and invest.

Setting Up Investment Accounts

Setting up your investment accounts is one of the most important steps in building long-term wealth. The type of account you choose determines not only how your money grows but also how it's taxed and how easily you can access it. By understanding the key account types and their benefits, you can make strategic decisions that align with your financial goals and timeline.

Employer-sponsored retirement accounts, such as 401(k), 403(b), and TSP plans, are among the most common ways to start investing. These accounts allow you to contribute pre-tax dollars, which means you lower your taxable income now while your investments grow tax-deferred until retirement. Many employers offer matching contributions, essentially free money, so it's crucial to contribute at least enough to capture the full match. Log in to your HR portal and review your plan details: Are you getting the full match? What investment options are available to you? Could you increase your contribution by even 1% this year? Small, consistent increases can make a significant impact over time.

If you don't have access to a workplace plan or want to invest beyond it, consider an **Individual Retirement Account (IRA)**. There are two main types: the Traditional IRA and the Roth IRA. A Traditional IRA lets you deduct your contributions from your taxes now, but you'll pay taxes when you withdraw the funds in retirement. A Roth IRA, on the other hand, doesn't provide an upfront tax break, but your withdrawals (including earnings) are tax-free in retirement. The best choice often depends on your expected tax rate: if you anticipate being in a higher bracket later, choose the Roth; if lower, the Traditional. Leading providers include Fidelity, Vanguard, Charles Schwab, M1 Finance, and Betterment, all of which offer user-friendly platforms and strong investment options.

Once you've maxed out your retirement contributions, open a **Taxable Brokerage Account** for more flexibility. Unlike retirement accounts, you can withdraw from these at any time without penalties, though you'll owe capital gains taxes on profits. These accounts are ideal for goals that don't fit into a retirement timeline, such as buying a home, starting a business, or reaching financial independence earlier. Great platforms for beginners include Fidelity for its all-around reliability, Charles Schwab for excellent service and low fees, SoFi Invest for its no-commission trades and cash bonuses, and Robinhood for its simple, beginner-friendly interface.

Finally, don't overlook **specialty accounts** that serve specific goals. A 529 Plan helps you save for education expenses with tax-free growth and withdrawals when used for qualified costs. A Health Savings Account (HSA) offers a rare triple tax advantage: contributions are tax-deductible, growth is tax-free, and withdrawals for medical expenses are tax-free. For parents and guardians, **custodial accounts** provide a powerful way to invest on behalf of a minor and teach children about money, and set them up for a stronger financial future.

Choosing the right mix of accounts gives you both flexibility and tax efficiency, ensuring your money works as hard and as smartly as possible toward your goals.

Technology for Investing

Technology has revolutionized how we invest, making it easier than ever to get started, automate decisions, and stay informed about your financial growth. Whether you prefer a hands-off approach or want to actively manage your portfolio, the right apps and platforms can make all the difference. The key is to choose tools that fit your comfort level, investing style, and long-term goals.

For those who prefer a hands-off experience, **robo-advisors** are an excellent place to begin. These automated investing platforms build and manage your portfolio based on your goals, risk tolerance, and timeline. If you prefer to take a more self-directed approach, several traditional brokerages offer powerful tools with minimal fees and excellent service.

Beyond investing platforms, using tracking and analysis tools helps you stay on top of your progress and make informed adjustments along the way. Whether you're just getting started or fine-tuning a complex portfolio, leveraging technology can help you invest smarter, track your progress effortlessly, and stay motivated as you build wealth over time.

How to Choose Investments That Fit You
Choosing investments that truly fit your needs requires a careful look at three key factors: your demographics, your psychology, and the resources you have available. Each of these elements influences how much risk you can take, which types of assets are most appropriate,

and how you can structure your portfolio for long-term success.

Your demographics, particularly your age, play a significant role in shaping your investment strategy. Younger investors, with decades ahead before retirement, can typically afford to focus on growth, allocating 80–90% of their portfolio to stocks to take advantage of compounding and long-term market gains. Older investors, on the other hand, often prioritize protecting their capital as they approach retirement. A portfolio of 40–60% stocks, with the remainder in bonds or cash, helps reduce volatility while still allowing for moderate growth.

Equally important are your psychographics, or your individual comfort level with risk. Risk-tolerant investors can weather market fluctuations and may choose growth-oriented assets such as stocks or real estate. Those who are more risk-averse often prefer stability, favoring bonds or balanced ETFs that offer steady returns with lower volatility. Additionally, socially conscious investors may opt for ESG (Environmental, Social, and Governance) funds, aligning their investments with their values while still pursuing growth.

Finally, the resources you have available, particularly the amount of money you can invest, will determine which accounts and investment vehicles make sense. For smaller amounts under $500, fractional-share investing platforms let you get started with minimal capital. Investors with $500 to $10,000 may benefit from robo-advisors, which provide automated portfolio management and guidance. For those with $10,000 or more, self-directed strategies, including ETFs, index funds, or even direct real estate investments, offer greater flexibility and growth potential.

By evaluating these three components, demographics, psychology, and resources, you can build a portfolio tailored to your unique situation, one that balances risk and reward while keeping you on track toward your long-term financial goals.

Building a Strong Investment Strategy
Building a strong investment strategy is essential for every investor, as it provides a clear framework for balancing risk and reward. Your strategy should reflect your financial goals, time horizon (timeframe before you need the invested money), and tolerance for market fluctuations. One approach is to consider sample portfolio allocations for different investor types.

A conservative investor, focused on protecting capital, might allocate 40% to stocks, 50% to bonds, and 10% to alternative investments. A balanced investor could hold 60% in stocks, 30% in bonds, and 10% in alternatives, aiming for moderate growth while managing risk. For those with a higher tolerance for market fluctuations and a longer time horizon, an aggressive investor might allocate 80% to stocks, 15%

to bonds, and 5% to alternative investments, seeking maximum growth potential.

Regardless of your allocation, it's important to rebalance your portfolio annually to maintain your target percentages and ensure your strategy continues to align with your goals. Market movements can shift your original allocation, and rebalancing helps you take profits from overperforming assets while investing more in underperforming areas, keeping your risk profile consistent over time.

Automation is another key element of a successful investment strategy. By setting up automatic deposits from your paycheck, you can ensure consistent contributions to your accounts without relying on willpower alone. Reinvesting dividends allows your earnings to compound, accelerating portfolio growth. Many modern platforms offer auto-rebalancing tools, which adjust your portfolio automatically to maintain your target allocation. These automated systems take the guesswork out of investing and foster a disciplined approach. After all, consistency is the foundation of wealth-building, and automation is one of the most effective ways to achieve it.

Retirement Planning and Timeline Adjustments
Planning for retirement requires more than just saving money. It requires a clear understanding of how much you will need and how your investment strategy should evolve over time. A helpful rule of thumb is the 5% Rule

(formerly the 4% rule), which provides a simple way to estimate the portfolio size needed to support your desired lifestyle. According to this rule, you can calculate your target portfolio by multiplying your expected annual spending by 20. For example, if you anticipate needing $60,000 per year in retirement, you would aim to accumulate a portfolio of approximately $1.2 million.

Your retirement strategy should also adjust based on how many years remain until you plan to retire. If you have more than 25 years before retirement, you can focus on aggressive growth, primarily investing in stocks and ETFs to take advantage of compounding and long-term market gains.

With 10 to 20 years remaining, a balanced approach is recommended, combining stocks and bonds to achieve growth while gradually reducing risk. If retirement is less than 10 years away, the focus should shift to preserving capital, emphasizing safer investments such as bonds, REITs, and cash equivalents to protect your nest egg from market volatility.

To refine your retirement plan and track your progress, several tools can be extremely helpful. Visualize different scenarios and adjust your savings strategy accordingly. By estimating your needs, adjusting your strategy over time, and leveraging planning tools, you can build a retirement plan that is both realistic and achievable.

Financial Independence, Retire Early

The Financial Independence, Retire Early (FIRE) movement has transformed the way people think about work and retirement. Instead of following the traditional path of working until age 65, FIRE advocates prioritize saving aggressively, investing wisely, and designing a lifestyle on their own terms. The movement is not one-size-fits-all; there are several variations depending on your goals and desired lifestyle.

Lean FIRE allows individuals to retire early while living a modest lifestyle, minimizing expenses to reach independence sooner. **Fat FIRE**, on the other hand, is designed for those who want to retire early with greater comfort and luxury, requiring a larger portfolio to sustain higher spending. **Barista FIRE** is a hybrid approach where individuals achieve partial financial independence and supplement their income by working part-time or in flexible roles. Finally, **Coast FIRE** focuses on investing heavily in the early years, allowing compounding growth to carry the portfolio forward without requiring large contributions later.

Achieving FIRE requires a disciplined approach. Core steps include
- saving 50–70% of your income,
- investing in low-cost index funds and real estate,
- eliminating high-interest debt, and
- consistently tracking your FI number.

Your FI number is your annual expenses multiplied by 25. This represents the amount needed to reach financial independence.

Several tools can support your journey. By combining aggressive saving, strategic investing, and careful planning, FIRE offers a path to live life on your own terms, potentially decades earlier than the traditional retirement timeline.

Alternative Wealth-Building Paths
Not everyone aspires to retire early, and that's perfectly fine. There are many alternative paths to building wealth that allow you to achieve financial security while maintaining flexibility and purpose. One option is **semi-retirement**, where you continue working part-time or consulting, providing income while freeing up time for other pursuits.

Cash flow investing focuses on acquiring assets that generate regular income, such as dividend-paying stocks or rental real estate, allowing your money to work for you while maintaining active involvement in your financial life.

Legacy investing takes a long-term view, building wealth not just for yourself but to transfer to future generations or donate to causes that matter to you, creating a lasting impact beyond your lifetime.

Finally, the **barbell strategy** balances your portfolio by combining ultra-safe investments with high-risk, high-reward opportunities, providing both security and growth potential.

Each of these approaches offers a unique way to grow wealth while aligning your investments with your personal goals, values, and lifestyle.

Keep Learning and Stay Consistent
Wealth-building is a journey. Keep your skills sharp and mindset strong. Continuously put money towards acquiring assets. The best investors aren't the smartest or luckiest; they're the most consistent. Don't wait until you "know everything." Every investor started with their first dollar, their first mistake, and their first lesson. Start today. Automate your success. Watch your wealth compound.

Chapter 17: Avoiding Burnout

Staying Energized on the Path to Financial Success – Avoiding Burnout and Maintaining Motivation

Achieving financial success is rarely a straight line. Paying off debt, saving diligently, and building wealth over time requires discipline, patience, and consistent action. But even the most committed individuals can experience burnout, a state of mental, emotional, and physical exhaustion that can slow progress, sap motivation, and even lead to setbacks.

Burnout often shows up as feelings of overwhelm, fatigue, or frustration. You might notice yourself avoiding budgeting tasks, skipping savings contributions, or rationalizing unnecessary spending just to feel a temporary sense of relief. If left unaddressed, burnout can make months or even years of progress feel wasted, and for some, it can lead to accumulating debt again, using savings, or missing key investment opportunities.

Why Avoiding Burnout Matters

Burnout isn't just uncomfortable. It can derail your financial journey. When you're mentally exhausted, decision-making suffers. Impulse spending increases. Saving and investing can feel like chores rather than empowering actions. The good news is that avoiding burnout is possible with mindful strategies and self-care. Protecting your energy is just as critical as protecting your money.

Self-Care Strategies for Financial Well-Being

Self-care is not a luxury. It's a necessity for success on your financial journey. Here are simple, practical ways anyone can stay energized and motivated:

1. **Celebrate Small Wins:** Paid off a credit card? Reached a savings milestone? Reward yourself in free or low-cost ways, such as having a favorite treat, a movie night, or an hour of leisure. Acknowledging progress fuels motivation.

2. **Set Realistic Goals:** Overly ambitious goals can lead to frustration. Break large financial objectives into smaller, achievable steps. Each step becomes a victory to celebrate.

3. **Schedule Money-Free Breaks:** Dedicate time to relax, pursue hobbies, or spend time with loved ones. Avoid thinking about finances constantly. Mental rest improves focus and decision-making.

4. **Maintain Physical Health:** Exercise, proper sleep, and balanced nutrition are good for the body and they help maintain emotional resilience and clarity for financial planning.

5. **Practice Mindful Spending:** Instead of depriving yourself completely, allow small, intentional spending that brings joy. Avoiding all pleasures can create feelings of scarcity and resentment.

The Role of a Financial Coach

A financial coach acts as both a guide and an accountability partner. They help you:

- Create realistic, personalized financial plans.

- Stay accountable to debt repayment, savings, and investment goals.
- Navigate emotional challenges, including stress and anxiety related to money.
- Identify and correct unhelpful patterns before burnout escalates.

Working with a financial coach can be particularly beneficial if you struggle to maintain consistency or feel so discouraged by setbacks that you stop taking action. They provide perspective, encouragement, and strategies to sustain progress.

Step-by-Step Strategy to Stay Motivated While Building Wealth

1. **Visualize Your Goals:** Keep your "why" front and center. Create a vision board, write a mission statement, or keep a journal of financial aspirations. Visual reminders reinforce commitment. Put the reminder where you will see it regularly.
2. **Break It Down:** Divide long-term goals (like paying off $50,000 in debt or building a $100,000 investment fund) into smaller monthly or weekly targets. Small successes compound motivation.
3. **Track Progress Consistently:** Use apps, spreadsheets, or journals to track spending, debt repayment, and investments. Seeing tangible progress, even minor. boosts morale.
4. **Create Accountability Systems:** Share your goals with a trusted friend, family member, or

financial coach. Regular check-ins reduce the temptation to procrastinate.

5. **Automate Where Possible:** Automate savings, bill payments, and investments to reduce mental load. Out of sight, out of mind—but still progressing.
6. **Reward Yourself Intentionally:** Set milestone rewards for achieving financial targets. Choose celebrations that reinforce success without derailing your plan.
7. **Practice Reflection:** Monthly, reflect on challenges and wins. Adjust strategies, refine goals, and remind yourself of the bigger picture.
8. **Seek Support When Needed:** Financial journeys can feel isolating. A coach, support group, or trusted community can provide advice, encouragement, and perspective.

Remember: Progress is a Marathon, Not a Sprint
Financial success is about building sustainable habits and making progress towards achieving financial goals. Avoiding burnout has to be strategic. Protect your energy, stay mindful, and seek support when needed. Each intentional step, no matter how small, brings you closer to the financial freedom you deserve.

Step 7: The Wealth Protection Blueprint

Chapter 18: Power of Insurance

Insurance plays a significant role in protecting wealth. In this chapter, we are going to discuss what insurance really is, what type of insurance you may need, and when you would need it.

What is insurance?

I know insurance usually gets a bad rap, and there is a lot of confusion around insurance. Some of this perception stems from "pushy" insurance agents. You may have encountered them: the ones who try to sell you something before learning about your financial situation. The ones who, after not asking real questions about your situation or proving that you can trust them, want you to write down the contact information for several friends so they can try to sell them something.

You should always feel comfortable talking to your financial planner about your money. If you don't get a good vibe or proper answers to your questions, then end the meeting. Say thanks for your time and get out of there, or show them out if the person is in your home.

The rest of the confusion can likely be blamed on the fact that financial literacy is not something that is highlighted in our communities or school system. Well, let's remove some of the confusion. Insurance is basically meant to protect your financial stability or the financial stability of your dependents.

Dependents are people (children and adults) who rely on you for financial support. If there is a large negative life event or disaster, if you will, insurance helps to protect you financially so that everything you're working so hard to establish doesn't come crashing down. Some also use insurance as one of their tools to ensure generational wealth.

There isn't a one-size-fits-all insurance solution. If you tried to look things up on your own, you know there is a plethora of options. The insurance you need fits your unique situation. There are numerous factors taken into consideration, such as the benefits you already receive from your employer, whether you have children, the number of children you have, your age, and your lifestyle.

Key Types of Insurance
There are also several different types of insurance that you need to cover different aspects of your life. The four main types of insurance you likely need are:
1. **Health** – protection against illness affecting your finances
2. **Life** – protection against death affecting your family or dependents' finances
3. **Car insurance** – protection against a car accident affecting your finances
4. **Long-term disability** – protection against disability affecting your finances

Let's go over each type in more detail, starting with life insurance.

Life insurance offers financial protection for your dependents or whoever you name as the beneficiary in the event of your death. If your income plays a major role in the survival and well-being of others, such as your spouse and children, then they would encounter financial hardship should you pass away. Getting life insurance would prevent them from having to go through financial hardship in that situation.

The general advice is to get a policy that is 10x your yearly income to cover household, funeral, childcare, and higher education expenses, and to provide a financial cushion. There are two major types of life insurance: **permanent life insurance** and **term life insurance**. The most common permanent life insurance types are whole life and universal life.

There are five things to consider when reviewing life insurance policies.

1. **The length or term:** the length of time, the specified number of years, of the policy
2. **The death benefit:** the amount of money that the insurance company will pay out
3. **The beneficiaries:** the person, people, or entity that receives the death benefit of the policy.
4. **The cash value:** a benefit of permanent life insurance policies that appreciates over time
5. **The premium:** the monthly or annual payments to maintain the policy

With whole life insurance, your policy remains in effect until your death. It never expires as long as you keep paying the premium. Your payments are invested, so you accumulate cash value that you can withdraw or borrow against. However, I do not recommend borrowing against it unless you have very strict criteria to mitigate potential problems. This is supposed to be protection against financial instability not adding to it. Also, the returns from the cash value component of whole life insurance aren't as good as those from other investment avenues. Upon your death, the payout goes to your named beneficiaries. This is the amount of the policy and any accumulated cash value.

The difference between whole life and universal life insurance is that universal life insurance has flexible premium payments. It also includes a cash value component and a death benefit.

With term life insurance, the insurance policy is valid until the agreed-upon term or length of time is reached. Of course, you still pay every month for the duration of that time. For example, say you get a twenty-year policy. You pay the premium for 20 years, and then the policy expires at that time. If your death occurs during those 20 years, then the agreed-upon amount in the policy is paid to your named beneficiaries.

Term life insurance typically costs less. It's renewable, but the rate you got when you started isn't renewed. You receive a new rate or cost based on your current factors, such as age, health conditions, lifestyle, and geographic location.

Which Life Insurance Do I Need?
Depending on your life and financial situation, as well as what you want to provide, that will determine if you should go with whole or term life insurance.

Term life insurance is good for young families who want to provide protection for their children or dependents in case something happens to the primary earners. It's also good if you know you only want the insurance coverage for a specific period of time. For example, say you took out a life insurance policy to cover your children and/or your spouse should something happen to you, but you feel they would no longer need that extra protection 20 or thirty years from now because at that point they would have accumulated enough of their own assets.

If you need coverage that lasts a lifetime, then you want to go with whole life or another type of permanent life insurance, such as universal life insurance. Universal life insurance is also great for those with variable or inconsistent income who would benefit from the ability to change the premium amount.

If you're the type of person who doesn't want to pay into a policy for so long that it will expire, then you may want to go with permanent life insurance. Also, if you want to be able to pass money from a policy on to your beneficiaries no matter what, then whole life insurance is also the way to go.

A good life insurance agent will help you take into consideration all the factors necessary to decide which is best for you. These will be your demographics as well as financial goals for yourself and your family.

Remember to update your policies after a big life event, such as a divorce, to make sure that the person named as the beneficiary is the person you want and need to get the money.

Health Insurance
Alright, let's move on to health insurance.

Health insurance helps you pay for healthcare. Even common procedures are way more expensive without health insurance. For example, in the U.S., the median cost to give birth in a hospital is around $30,000, and if you have to get a caesarean section, then the bill will be closer to $38,000. Could you imagine having to come up with all that money to pay a hospital bill after just having a baby? With health insurance, you only pay a certain percentage of the bill.

In America, healthcare is private, which means that, after complying with federal and state laws, each company can set its own rules for how and when it will cover healthcare costs. This is why you have to shop around and assess different insurance plans and companies to find the one that fits your needs.

Health Insurance Plans
The plans you can choose from are based on the marketplaces available to you. This breaks down into four different options.

1) Employer marketplace
If you are employed full-time with benefits, your employer shows you the available plans. You likely receive a benefits package from HR or the benefits department when it's time to re-enroll in your insurance package.

2) Government exchange
If you do not receive employer-sponsored insurance benefits, another option is to use the government marketplace.

3) Private exchange
Another option, if you do not get health insurance benefits from your employer, is to use a private exchange.

4) Individual Insurer
The fourth option is to pick an insurance company and use one of its offered plans.

The cheapest option is usually the insurance offered by your employer, since the employer pays some of the costs.

When you're analyzing the available plans, there should be a chart that summarizes their benefits so you can compare them. Using the chart and in-depth descriptions, you can see what's included under each and pick the coverage that's best for you and your family.

The things to think about as you consider a plan are:
- Do you need or want coverage for providers out of network? This is where the insurance covers a portion of the costs if you need or want to see a physician who is outside of your network. The network is the list of physicians and facilities that partner with that insurer.
- Are there locations that are relatively close to you?
- Also consider if you will need a referral from your PCP to see a specialist. Is that something you don't mind, or do you want to be able to see a specialist as necessary without a referral?

Think about this as you review different plans.

Types of Insurance Plans
There are four types of insurance plans: HMOs, PPOs, EPOs, and POS

1) HMO: Health Maintenance Organization

You pick a PCP (primary care physician). Your PCP coordinates all your care, since you need referrals from the PCP to see specialists. These specialists will also be in-network so that you have insurance coverage. Out-of-network physicians or providers are not covered, unless it is an emergency. The out-of-pocket costs are usually lower than with the other plans.

2) PPO: Preferred Provider Organization

With this type of plan, you do not need a referral from a PCP to visit another physician or specialist. You can visit any physician; however, an in-network physician, also called a provider, will be cheaper and more likely to be covered by the insurance. When you visit an out-of-network physician, the costs are less likely to be covered and may be entirely out of pocket.

3) EPO: Exclusive Provider Organization

Under this type of plan, the insurer will only cover costs for visits to network physicians. There is no out-of-network except for emergencies.

4) POS: Point of Service

This plan is like a mix of the HMO and PPO plans. For example, plans may require you to choose a PCP who must provide referrals to specialists. However, you can see out-of-network physicians, but you may incur more costs.

The next significant factor in choosing a health insurance plan type is cost.   Consider:

1) The premium – This is the monthly payment to maintain insurance coverage.

2) The deductible – This is the amount that you need to pay before the insurance company will cover the costs.

3) The copay – The copayment is the amount you pay when you go in for a service before reaching the deductible for some costs, like preventative care, and after reaching your deductible for others. Usually, the copay ranges from $15 - $30.

4) Out-of-pocket maximum - This is the maximum amount you pay for services, e.g., copays and the deductible go towards this maximum. Once the maximum is reached then the insurance will pay 100% of costs.

Here's a cheat table:

Plan Type	Out-of-network coverage	Need a referral to specialists	Costs Expectation
HMO	No, only emergencies	Yes	Lower
PPO	Yes	No	Higher

EPO	No, only emergencies	No	Lowest
POS	Yes	Yes	Higher

Which Type of Health Insurance Plan Is Best For You

1) HMO is good if you want lower premiums and out-of-pocket costs. If you want a primary care physician to coordinate your care, even if you need to see specialists, then an HMO may be the way to go.

2) PPO is good if you want to be able to see specialists without getting referrals from a PCP. Also, if you want the option to see out-of-network physicians, this is a good option. The costs will be higher, but your insurer may provide some coverage.

3) EPO is a good option for you if you want lower premiums and out-of-pocket costs, but still want the option to be able to see specialists without a referral. Remember, they will still need to be in-network.

4) POS is a good option if you still want a primary care physician (PCP) to coordinate your care, but you also want the option to see out-of-network specialists. Again, the cost will be higher, but your insurer may provide some coverage.

Car Insurance

Ok, let's talk about car insurance. Car insurance is to protect you and any other person who may be involved in a car accident from financial ruin. We discussed the cost of a car and the fact that you likely do not have the money lying around to simply run out and fix a car or get a new one. Remember that's the purpose of insurance, protecting your financial stability.

There are different types of car insurance. As you're trying to decide what car insurance plan you need, it's important to understand the different insurance coverage types. Not all are mandatory. Check your state laws to determine which coverage is required.

Types of Car Insurance
1) Uninsured/Underinsured Coverage
This is when there is an accident that is not your fault, and the other driver involved is not insured. The coverage usually includes vehicle repairs, medical bills, and funeral costs if you had passengers.

2) Collision Coverage
This covers vehicle repairs if you're in an accident. If the car is a total loss, you'll receive a payment equal to its full value.

3) Bodily Injury Liability Coverage
This covers bodily harm that befalls your passengers, the passengers in other cars, and injured bystanders in

a car accident. It will cover medical bills, funeral expenses, legal fees, and pain and suffering expenses.

4) Property Damage Liability Coverage

This covers any property damage to the area surrounding the accident site, as well as damage to other cars involved in the accident. With this coverage, damage to your vehicle is NOT covered.

5) Comprehensive Coverage

This coverage pays for damages to your car that are not caused by a car accident. Let's say your car was broken into or stolen, then comprehensive coverage would cover the costs. You're also covered for things like natural disasters.

Picking Car Insurance

In general, that is what each type of car insurance covers; however, for any insurance you're considering, remember to read the details. Each company may have differences in what's covered.

Most states make bodily injury liability coverage and property damage liability coverage mandatory, so check the laws for your state.

When shopping for car insurance:
- Check out the company to make sure there aren't a lot of complaints against them and that they are in good financial standing. You want to make sure

they can actually pay if you do need to, and that they treat their customers well.

- Get clear on what's covered to make sure you have enough coverage for your lifestyle.
- Be clear on whether they cover out-of-state accidents if you travel out of state with your car
- Compare the rewards and discounts that are available. You may be able to get a deal based on meeting certain safety requirements or having a good driving record.
- Determine if you bundle different types of insurance, like your home and car insurance, and if you can get a discount or great deal.

Anytime there is a major life shift, re-evaluate your insurance coverage. You may be eligible for a lower rate. For example, if you've moved to a new zip code, have gone a few years without any violations or accidents, have graduated to a new age bracket, etc.

Long-term Disability
You may be thinking, "I'm young. I won't need this." Or "I don't have a dangerous job, so I don't need this." Well, let me break it down. When we talked about emergency funds, I said, "Things happen." Unexpected things happen. The same can be said here. According to the US Social Security Administration, a 20-year-old has a 1 in 4 chance of becoming disabled before retirement, while they still need to work to survive.

223

According to the Council for Disability Awareness, 95% of causes for disability and illness are not work-related, so they are not covered by workers' comp, also known as workers' compensation insurance. The average long-term disability claim is for 34.6 months. Almost three years is a LONG time to be unable to work to pay your bills. Would you be able to cover your household bills for nearly three years?

Depending on your situation, you may be able to cover it, such as if your spouse has enough income to pay the bills, or a mix of other insurance savings and income can cover it. However, if the answer is no, absolutely not, then you may want to consider long-term disability insurance.

Many employers offer this to employees. Check with your benefits office or human resources department. If your employer does not offer long-term disability insurance or what is offered is not enough, you can purchase it from a private provider.

After your short-term disability is used up, long-term disability applies. Short-term disability usually lasts 3-6 months. Long-term disability insurance will usually pay 50-60% of your salary until you are well enough to go back to work or until the policy expires, in other words, you've reached the agreed-upon amount of time in the policy.

If you get the insurance through your employer, who pays the premium before taxes are deducted, you will have to pay taxes on the benefits. If you're paying the premium yourself with after-tax dollars, you won't be taxed on the income, the benefits.

Social security does pay some benefits for those who become disabled, but the program has very strict eligibility requirements, and the monthly payout is low. You can collect Social Security Disability benefits from a private provider.

Your income is necessary for survival and to build wealth, so protect it.

Chapter 19:
Importance of Wills

In this chapter, we are going to discuss what a will really is, what it does, and how to create one.

What Is a Will?

A will, also known as a last will and testament, is basically an instruction manual as to what to do with the things you own when you pass away. To avoid fighting among family members and ensure things are handled the way you want, you need to leave instructions.

You may have heard the term estate planning. Well, a will is part of that process. Your estate is all the money, assets, and property you own. The will lays out how your estate should be distributed to your beneficiaries. Usually, the beneficiaries are family members, but can be anyone or entity of your choosing. Sometimes a person will pass some or all of their estate to different charities.

A Legal Will

The laws governing what must be in place for a will to be legal and binding can vary from state to state. Your will must adhere to the laws of the state and cannot leave instructions that try to circumvent or ignore state laws. It's best to work with an attorney to help write the will.

However, here are some general rules. You must be of sound mind when the will was created. This means you clearly understood what you were doing and saying, and that you were not coerced or manipulated by anyone.

Wills can be written or typed. They must be notarized. This is where a notary signs and certifies the document as legal. A notary is a person who is authorized to certify documents.

Other Types of Wills
There are two other types of wills, but they are not recognized in every state.
1) Holographic – a holographic will is handwritten and was signed without witnesses. Only some states recognize this as a valid will.

2) Nuncupative – a nuncupative will is an oral will. It's not accepted in every state, and the ones that do accept this will typically have specific rules for it to be allowed. For example, if you are unable to write a will because of a sudden illness, then a nuncupative will may be allowed.

What Can It Do?
Here are the main things you can include in a will.

1) You can dictate what happens to your belongings and real estate.
Any property that you want to leave with specific instructions on how it should be distributed can be included in your will. You can detail how the estate can be given to your heirs and beneficiaries.

Of course, this is a great thing to do, as it prevents arguments stemming from different opinions among family members about what should happen to your things, your home, your money, etc. My suggestion is to include everything, even if you think no one is going to care or fight over what would happen to that item.

Leave instructions on options to handle your clothes, jewelry, musical instruments, etc. These are all examples I've heard have caused major family rifts after a family member dies.

2) Appoint a guardian for your children or any dependent who will need a guardian.
Have a conversation with any potential guardian prior to naming them in the will. This way, you ensure they are comfortable with the idea and can step in if ever needed. Those movies that show adults encountering some situation where they have to randomly take over the care of a child they didn't know about, or didn't know they were named as the guardian, are cute. But unrealistic, and it's better to avoid that scenario.

Remember, this works with the other laws of your state and the federal law. Therefore, you cannot use a will to try to circumvent parental rights or anything of that nature.

3) Appoint the executor.
This is the person or institution that ensures the instructions in the will are carried out. You want to make sure you pick someone or an institution that will carry out the instructions in the will accurately. Usually,

people choose a family member or an institution such as a bank.

Some of the things that the executor will need to do are:
- Start the probate process. This involves filing papers with the court to verify that the will is valid, aka real and legal
- Take inventory of your estate
- Pay off any outstanding bills and taxes
- Handle funeral costs
- Notify government institutions such as social security and the post office
- Cancel all subscriptions and notify banks
- Distribute the estate in accordance to the will

If you pick a person, rather than an institution, make sure this is someone who is well-organized, pays attention to detail, is honest, and is dependable. You want to feel confident that they will get all those duties done efficiently. Also, check with the laws for your state. There may be laws with special requirements for different scenarios, such as if the person is out of state or if the beneficiaries are children.

Make sure to have a conversation with this person before naming them as the executor. Also, let them know where the financial and other documents are that they will need to do their duties.

4) Donate to charities.

If you want to make sure some or all eligible funds and property from your estate go to your favorite charity, then you can outline that in your will.

Consider causes that you care about and name the specific nonprofit organization in your will. If the nonprofit is a 501(c) (3) organization, you may reduce the taxes your beneficiary has to pay.

There are three types of taxes that they may need to pay: inheritance taxes, estate taxes, and income taxes. Not all states collect inheritance taxes.

An **inheritance tax** is the amount the beneficiary must pay based on the value of the property they inherit under the will. An **estate tax** is a tax that the estate must pay before beneficiaries receive assets. There can be federal and state estate taxes.

When you donate to a charity, you support a cause you care about and reduce the tax burden for the beneficiaries.

Writing a Will
To write your will, you have three options.

1) Write, really type, it yourself.
You'll need to make sure you're familiar with your state laws regarding wills. If you're not crystal clear on all the laws, you may want to get help. If anything in your will

231

isn't in accordance with the federal and state laws where you reside, your will won't be valid.

2) You can use an online program to walk you through the process.

There are a number of options. Get recommendations from trusted family and friends. Also, do an internet search to see what is currently available.

3) You can hire an attorney to help you write a will

that is in accordance with state and federal laws. Pick someone with experience writing wills and who knows the laws of your state. Remember, each state may have different laws, so if you use an attorney, then you need one licensed in your state.

If your will and testament will be straightforward, you may opt to write it yourself or use an online program. Here is a simplified version of the process and some key pieces of information that you will need to include.

1) Name your beneficiaries or heirs.

In the majority of states, your spouse can legally inherit and you cannot disinherit or cut them out using your will. You will have to hire an attorney to see what if anything can be done in your case if you do not want anything going to your spouse for some reason.

After major life events, remember to update your listed beneficiaries on things such as your retirement accounts etc. You don't want someone you divorced 30 years ago to get the money when you've already been re-married for quite some time. You just forgot to update the beneficiary paperwork.

2) Name the executor.
Remember this is the person who makes sure the instructions of the will get carried out.

3) Name guardians.
If you have children or other dependents, and their other biological or adoptive parent also passed, then you can name who their guardian will be.

4) Explain the distribution of your property.
Here property is not just real estate. Property is anything you owned. Remember above when I said dictate what should happen to clothes and jewelry too. The clothes and jewelry also count as property.

5) Sign the will and get it notarized.
This means you get it legalized by a notary. A notary is a person who has been certified by the state to deem a document a legal valid document. They will verify your identity. Make sure you're signing on your own free will. The notary's seal is to serve as evidence that it is an authentic and valid document.

6) Your witnesses sign the will.
The number of witnesses depends on your state law. You usually need 2-3 witnesses. The witnesses cannot be beneficiaries under the will. If the will is contested, then the witness

can state that they saw a person of sound mind sign the will.

The procedure will be something like what is explained above; check with your state. You have to declare to the witnesses that they are about to watch you sign your will. Then you sign it, likely in front of a notary. Then the witnesses sign it.

7) Provide it to the executor or a law office that will provide it to the executor upon your death.

Chapter 20: Power of Attorney

In this chapter, we are going to discuss what the power of attorney is, what it does, and when you need it.

What is the power of attorney?

You may have heard of this term. You may not have. I think the first time I heard of it, well, that I can remember, was while watching a TV show. The family was in the hospital, and then someone asked about a Power of Attorney to make a decision about treatment. I don't remember how old I was, but from that, I assumed that was something you needed if you were in the hospital. That's not quite right. Have you had a similar experience?

A power of attorney is a document that grants someone the authority to act on behalf of another person. The person to whom authority has been granted is called the agent. They can be granted complete autonomy, or their authority can be limited to specific fields or situations. The person requiring the power of attorney is called the principle.

When Is It Needed?

There are various reasons why you could need a Power of Attorney. Some examples are:
- If you're out of the country or have another reason why you cannot be physically present to sign legal documents
- If you're really sick or have been diagnosed with a severe illness
- If you're disabled and unable to sign documents

These are just a few examples of situations where you would use a power of attorney, whether you're the agent or the principle.

Even if you're relatively young, this will become very important not only for you, but perhaps also for your parents. Many adults in their 30s and 40s end up caring for their children and their parents at the same time. That's why they call it the sandwich generation, sandwiched in between their parents and children. In this scenario, you're working on building wealth while taking care of two different groups of people. You may also need a power of attorney to help parents manage their wealth as medical bills rise.

Types of Power of Attorney
There are two main types of power of attorney: general and special or limited

1) General Power of Attorney
The general Power of Attorney grants broad authority to act in various situations on behalf of the principal. This person or institution can make financial and health decisions.

2) Limited Power of Attorney
A limited power of attorney will restrict authority to a single area. For example, a health care or medical power of attorney would authorize someone to make the decisions regarding your health care while you're

unconscious or if you're mentally unable to make the decisions on your own.

You may also need to create a Durable Power of Attorney. This is a document used when you already have a power of attorney and basically says that if you become mentally incompetent, then your current power of attorney remains valid.

When Does It Start?

A Power of Attorney goes into effect upon signing or in a pre-determined situation, such as disability or when you become mentally incompetent. You have to be of sound mind when it is created and signed.

The Agent

An agent acting under a power of attorney must keep excellent records of everything done for the principal. Same as with picking an executor of a will, you want to choose someone that you trust, someone who is organized and can keep good records. This person should have your very best interests at heart.

When you appoint an agent, consider having a backup in case your agent becomes ill or goes through a circumstance that makes it impossible to perform their agent duties. The backup can then fill in for the original agent.

If you're considering having multiple agents, make sure to pick people who will work well together. They will likely have to work together at some point. Make sure there isn't anyone with a very busy schedule who could delay decisions.

Alright, now that you know about a power of attorney, how do you draft one if needed? Well, you can write it up yourself, just like a will. However, it would benefit you to speak to an attorney and get advice on what powers to authorize and what language should be in the power of attorney.

You will also have to get your power of attorney notarized. You have to make copies of the notarized document for institutions that the agent may need to use on your behalf. For example, your bank or credit union will need a copy of the notarized document.

Keep track of which institutions receive a copy of the power of attorney. If you revoke it, which you can do at any time with a notarized Revocation of Power of Attorney document, you will need to get back all the copies. You'll have to notify the agent in writing and notify any necessary institutions.

Chapter 21: Elevated for Life

Wealth Maintenance & Mastery Plan

If you've made it to this point, pause for a moment. Not because there is so much more work to do, but because something important has already happened. You are no longer *starting* your financial journey. You are maintaining it.

That distinction matters more than most people realize. Many people spend years cycling through financial advice, restarting budgets, resetting goals, and "trying again" every January. What keeps them stuck isn't a lack of knowledge. It's a lack of systems and identity. They are constantly chasing, fixing, or reacting to a financial crisis. You are no longer in that phase.

You now have a financial framework that is designed to work with real life, not against it. You've built structure, clarity, and intention around how money flows into your life, how it is managed, how it grows, and how it is protected. That is what elevates wealth from something fragile into something sustainable. Wealth is built by quiet consistency, not dramatic moments. Lottery winner announcements are sensational. However, the chance of winning millions or billions is remote. Consistently executing wealth-building habits over time is what truly builds wealth for the average person.

It's a System: How the 7 Steps Work Together

Each step in this book was intentionally designed to build upon the previous one, not as isolated actions, but as a living system.

You began with organization, because clarity always comes before control. You shifted your mindset because behavior follows belief. You learned how to design and maintain a realistic budget for direction. You implemented systems so your money could function even when your motivation fluctuated. You learned how to leverage credit wisely, rather than be controlled by it. You prepared for financial independence in a way that honors both growth and rest. And finally, you protected what you're building so your wealth can last beyond today, beyond you.

Individually, these steps are powerful. Together, they create stability. This is what allows your finances to reach a state of balance, where progress doesn't depend on constant effort, and where setbacks don't erase momentum. When one part of the system is temporarily stressed, the rest of the system supports it. That intentional design helps mitigate financial disaster.

Your Annual Wealth Reset Protocol
Wealth does not require daily obsession, but it does require periodic intention. Just as your body benefits from regular checkups, your finances benefit from a simple, predictable rhythm of review, analysis and adjustment. This is how you prevent minor issues from becoming major disruptions.

Think in terms of resets, not restarts.

- **Monthly**, you check in with your cash flow and systems. Compare your actual spending to your plan and make adjustments as necessary.
- **Quarterly**, you revisit goals, debt progress, and savings alignment to ensure your money still reflects your priorities.
- **Annually**, you conduct a complete wealth reset:
    - Review insurance coverage
    - Check your credit report
    - Revisit wills and powers of attorney
    - Adjust savings and investment contributions as income changes
    - Analyze your debt elimination progress

This rhythm keeps your wealth momentum responsive, not reactive. You stay ahead of problems without living in constant vigilance. The goal is regulation, not perfection.

Wealth Without Burnout
One of the most overlooked aspects of financial success is energy. Burnout doesn't just come from working too hard. It comes from making too many decisions, carrying too much uncertainty, and feeling like your finances require constant attention. That's why systems matter. Automation matters. Simplicity matters.
Wealth should reduce mental strain, not increase it.
As you move forward, give yourself permission to stop over-optimizing. Not every decision needs to be maximized. Not every dollar needs to be perfectly placed. "Good and consistent" will outperform "perfect

but exhausting" every time. A truly wealthy life includes rest, margin, and ease.

When Life Happens and It Will

No financial system exists in a vacuum. Careers change. Families grow. Health shifts. Economies fluctuate. Unexpected expenses will still happen, not because you failed, but because life is dynamic. The difference now is that you are no longer financially fragile.

You don't have to panic, desperately use debt, abandon your plan, or start over. You adjust. You adapt. You use the framework you've built to make informed decisions rather than emotional ones. This is what financial resilience looks like. Wealth isn't about avoiding disruption, as that's impossible and unrealistic. It's about having the capacity to absorb it and prevent disruption from turning into a disaster.

Teaching Wealth Forward

At some point, wealth stops being just about you. Whether you have children, a partner, extended family, or a community that watches how you move through the world, your financial behavior becomes a form of leadership. People learn more from what you model than from what you explain. Calm decision-making. Preparedness instead of panic. Consistency instead of extremes. Wealth-building habits are on display day in and day out. This is how wealth becomes generational, not only in money, but in mindset. Teach and show the next generation how to add to the wealth, not just use it up.

Your Next Level

As your finances stabilize, your needs will evolve. You may find yourself wanting more personalization, more strategic guidance, or tools that reduce friction even further. That's not a sign that what you've built isn't working. It's a sign that you're ready for refinement. Growth doesn't mean complexity. You can keep things simple and adjust for alignment with your current level. Move forward at a pace that supports your lifestyle, not one that competes with it.

Wealth Really Is Simple

Simple is not the same as easy. Building wealth is not easy, but simple. Simple enough to be repeated. Simple enough to be sustained. Keep doing the right things consistently, calmly, and with intention. You are no longer chasing wealth. You are directing and growing it.

And that is what elevates everything.

RESOURCES:

For tools to help implement the protocol explained in this book, go to pocketofmoney.com/wise-resources.